GOD AND BIBLE

Exploring Stories from
Genesis to Job

Antony F. Campbell, SJ

PAULIST PRESS
New York/Mahwah, NJ

The scripture quotations are from the NRSV unless otherwise noted.

Cover design by Joy Taylor
Book design by Lynn Else

Library of Congress Cataloging-in-Publication Data

Campbell, Antony F.
    God and Bible : exploring stories from Genesis to Job / Antony F. Campbell.
        p.   cm.
    ISBN 978-0-8091-4520-1 (alk. paper)
    1. Bible stories, English—O.T. I. Title.
BS550.3.C35 2008
220.6—dc22
                                                        2007044657

Published by Paulist Press
997 Macarthur Boulevard
Mahwah, New Jersey 07430

www.paulistpress.com

Printed and bound in the
United States of America

Contents

CONTENTS

Acknowledgments

The initiative that triggered these pieces came via an invitation from Andrew Bullen, SJ, at that time editor of *Madonna* magazine. In the process of revision, the book has been licked into shape with immensely valuable input from Larry Boadt, CSP, and Paul McMahon of Paulist Press. I am deeply grateful to all three. My sincere thanks also to Nicole Rotaru who provided the suggestions for the Reflective Activity sections.

Dedicated to all lovers of a good story

Introduction

Debunking has had its day. Much of modern science has become part of our everyday world. Biblical scholarship—with ancient languages and literatures, archaeology, geography, and history, and so much more—has risen to sometimes dizzying heights and descended to sometimes almost bewilderingly arcane depths. It is time to take all this on board and return to the delights of wide-eyed reading of Older Testament texts, untrammeled by outworn specters from bygone days.

Long read as "how it was," the early stories of Genesis make good sense when freed to be read as reflections on "how it is and always has been" (part one). The ancestral stories of Israel have long been read through the lens of sons and land (thanks to Gen 15 and 17); at least the possibly older traditions need to be read in quest of other meanings (part two). Where Israel's presence in Canaan is concerned, the initial half of the Book of Joshua, hedged in by the promises to the ancestors, was characterized first as portraying *conquest,* then *occupation,* then *infiltration,* and then *peasant revolt*—with the mysteries of the book still unplumbed and its interpretation still unresolved; once Israel is in possession of the land, the theological reflection in the Book of Judges needs to be given its due (part three). The stories of David have often been told; their insight and sophistication have too often been neglected (part four). The prophets, in various guises, have long been favorites; the selections chosen are intended to make even clearer the attraction of the prophets for us today (parts five and six).

It is along the lines of these convictions that this book has been put together. At its core are texts and stories given page-length treatment over some years in an Australian devotional magazine, *Madonna*, in a series entitled "Full of Surprises." The theme of surprise will recur frequently enough. The space available restricted discussion to not much more than six hundred words or so. Brevity's advantages still outweigh its disadvantages so expansion has usually been resisted and succinctness sustained. Brevity helps make stories easier to grasp and texts easier to understand.

Many of these biblical texts or stories raise questions or discreetly leave issues open for reflection. Highlighting these, without closing them off with answers, is not a matter of being coy or withholding insight. Personal reflection is important and needs to come from each of us. All of us are invited to reflect; our own reflections have a worth for each of us as believers that ought not be preempted.

Our own reflections have to be honest. Where we find good, we rejoice; where we do not, it may require courage to accept our own belief. Yet only in honesty can we come close to God. The hope of this book is to give the Bible back to itself and enable us to appreciate it and see its value.

This book is free of any academic apparatus or scholarly references. Readers interested in pursuing matters further may wish to consult the following, where ample references to the literature can be found.

For parts one and two: Antony F. Campbell and Mark A. O'Brien, *Sources of the Pentateuch* (Fortress, 1993), *Rethinking the Pentateuch* (Westminster John Knox, 2005).

For part three: Campbell and O'Brien, *Unfolding the Deuteronomistic History* (Fortress, 2000) and Campbell, *Joshua to Chronicles* (Westminster John Knox, 2004).

For part four: Campbell, *1 Samuel* and *2 Samuel* (Eerdmans, 2003 and 2005).

For parts five and six: Campbell, *Of Prophets and Kings* (Catholic Biblical Association of America, 1986) and also Campbell, *Study Companion to Old Testament Literature* (Glazier/Liturgical Press, 1989/1992). More recently: David L. Petersen, *The Prophetic Literature: An Introduction* (Westminster John Knox, 2002) and Marvin A. Sweeney, *The Prophetic Literature* (Abingdon, 2005).

As companion to this and the above, from Paulist Press, there is, of course, Campbell, *God First Loved Us: The Challenge of Accepting Unconditional Love* (2000).

Also, from Eerdmans (2008) there is Campbell, *The Whisper of Spirit: A Believable God Today*.

PART ONE:
Revealed Beginning or Pondered Present

OURSELVES AND OUR GOD

Introduction

The six-day creation account at the start of Genesis has long been identified in the popular mind with *the* biblical image of creation, overwhelmingly dominant as the Bible's portrayal of how this world began. Genesis 1 is most imposing, both stylistically and from the point of view of location. Nevertheless, a glance at the other widely different biblical texts involving creation makes it patently obvious that the notion that Genesis 1 gives *the* single dominant view of creation advanced in the Bible is absolute nonsense. That the idea has survived so long and is so widespread is witness to a reverence for the Bible that does not necessarily correlate with reading it closely, or—possibly worse—the extent to which traditional belief has controlled the understanding of biblical text. Churches, communities, and individuals are entitled to their beliefs, but they should look closely before attributing them to the Bible.

Beyond the creation issue, and to an extent freed from the weight of theological tradition, the question that biblical scholarship has to ask itself is whether the stories placed early in Genesis (Gen 2—11) reveal how it was thought to have been back then, *at* the beginning, or whether they portray how it is now (in the authors' day and ours) and has always been, *from* the very beginning. It is clear that ancient Israel had a number of ways of picturing the process of creation. Is it possible that ancient Israel told a number of stories of human life as it was and had always been? If so, it is not surprising that Israel's compilers chose to put these stories at the beginning of the Bible; it is where the human life portrayed began. Close inspection shows that they are not suitable as a revelation of how it was *at* the beginning (they offer options, provide conflicting information, etc.); rather, they reveal the outcome of later pondering—how humankind has always been, *from* the beginning.

We cannot allow ourselves to indulge in whimsy or what we as moderns might like to think was the case, powered by modern prejudice or wishful thinking. When interpreting any text, we can only deal in the detailed evidence found in the text itself, a quality of argument that would stand up under the best of careful scrutiny. Interpretation, the making of meaning for texts, is an art; by definition, it cannot be definitive. What we have the right to be definite about is what these early texts in Genesis—on their own evidence—are not: they are not a portrayal of how it was thought to have been back then, at the beginning. The evidence is there in the ancient text.

Because it is important, we need to lay out the hard evidence in some detail; what follows can be heavy going for some readers. If it is for you, skip to the conclusion. To anticipate that conclusion right here: these early stories in Genesis did not tell Israel and do not tell us how it was back then at the beginning, or even how it was thought to have been back then at the beginning. That leaves us with the very big question: why tell them then? What did they mean? What do they mean?

The Garden story (2:4b—3:24) cannot tell us or them how it was thought to have been back then at the beginning, because it offers the option of at least two quite different stories about that beginning. We all know there were two trees in the garden, the tree of life and the tree of the knowledge of good and evil (2:9). But the story told in detail refers to "the tree that is *in the middle* of the garden" (3:3). That is not helpful if there are two trees in the middle. As one friend said to the other: Why don't you sit inside my car, out of the rain, and wait for me; the car's not locked and I won't be long. Said the second: where is your car? Reply: in the middle of the parking lot. Said the other: but I can see the parking lot and there are two cars in the middle. Said the friend: mine is the Ford. Said the second: but they're both Fords. Said the friend: mine's red. Said the other: sorry, but they're both red. Said the friend: I don't believe this; just a minute and I'll come with you. So with two trees in the middle of the garden, there is the possibility of two stories to be told. A second observation supports this. The story that is told in detail is told about a couple, the man and the woman. At the end of chapter 3, three verses name the man only and lest he "reach out his hand and take also from the tree of life...the Lord God sent him forth from the garden" (3:22–23). Perhaps the woman was included with the man; perhaps the woman did not feature at all in this version of the story. All we know for certain is that the text makes clear to us that we do not know how it was back then, at the beginning.

As a text of theological significance, portraying a single event in the life of the first human couple, this story (Gen 2:4b—3:24) has long been treated as etiological, explaining the presence of evil in the world. The argument was: human life as we know it is out of joint with the purposes of God; some human calamity must have triggered the immense disorder we now see around us. However, there is a huge difference in meaning between portraying the *cause* of what is and portraying the insightful *observation* of what is—that is, aware of boundaries, humans have always tended to overstep them and incur consequences. The cause (etiology) claims to tell us *why* life is the way it is; the observation (experience) tells us *that* life is the way it is—and has been from the beginning. Such stories invite us to see what we are like, to be more acutely aware of the regrettable human capacity constantly to make life hard for ourselves. Perhaps the narrative was meant to be etiological, but the text does not provide support for such a meaning; in the text, the consequences of the acts of the couple in the Garden are not portrayed extending beyond the story. To the contrary, it may be that we are to blame for our own failures. It may be that ancient Israel was too smart to pass the buck and blame others in the distant past. Rather than etiological, the text may be educational (raising children and producing food embrace the whole), an example of how life is and has been from the start—and will continue to be if we don't wise up.

Some languages distinguish singular and plural address (English: thou, thee, thy; you, you, your; French: *tu, vous;* German: *du, Sie;* Spanish: *tu, ustedes;* etc.); others do not. In English the distinction has largely lapsed; it is used in certain ecclesiastical and liturgical contexts or is now archaic or poetic. In Hebrew, the distinction between singular and plural address is maintained. In the Hebrew biblical text, the address to both man and woman is in the singular, speaking of the two individuals and not of the rest of us—harder work for him and more painful childbirth for her. There is no reference to consequences for the rest of us, beyond an enmity between snakes and future humans, spelled out quite emphatically (3:15). It would have been so easy to add clauses in verse 16 and at the end of verse 17 pointing to the future; there are no such clauses. In fact, "you shall eat the plants of the field" (v. 18) applies only to life before the Flood when vegetarianism was the rule (for after the Flood, see 9:2–3). The report of the births of Cain and Abel (4:1–2; also Seth and Enosh, 4:25–26) has no trace of any awareness of 3:16; the vocation of Cain (tiller of the ground, 4:2) does not show any sign of awareness of 3:17. In the case of both the man and woman, there is no reference to generations to come, such as for ancestors and the promises made them; there is no reference to descendants, such as is usual for kings and their dynasties. What is said about childbearing being much more painful and toil being more burdensome is in the singular, clearly addressed to the two individuals, the woman and the man, respectively. It may be that it was understood as addressed only to them and not to the rest of us; maybe not original sin but a portrayal of the first example of natural sin. We do it; they did it.

The two stories that follow, one of Cain and his brother (4:1–16) and the other of Cain and his descendants (4:17–24), clearly do not tell us how it was thought to have been back then. Condemned by God for killing Abel, Cain complains that "anyone who meets me may kill me" (4:14). According to the text, there was only his mom and dad. Having sired a son, Enoch, Cain built a city. Hardly intended to portray how it was back then; there were only the three of them—Cain, wife, and son. On the other hand, a city is a major step toward civilization. In the seventh generation within this story (Cain to Enoch to Irad to Mehujael to Methushael to Lamech to Jabal, Jubal, and Tubal-cain), further steps toward civilization are listed.

The symbolism of development is present. It began with Cain and the city, here possibly inimical to God (cf. Babel: city and tower). Seven generations down the track, credit as the originators of three great strands of civilization is given to Jabal for the pastoral industry (tents and livestock), Jubal for music (lyre and pipe), and Tubal-cain for metallurgy (bronze and iron). Perhaps violence and metalworking (technology) go hand in hand. Cain was promised sevenfold vengeance (4:15); Lamech, father of Tubal-cain, claims seventy-sevenfold vengeance (4:24). The association of violence with technology is not said; it may be suspected. Certainly, violence is on the increase.

Once again, with the Flood, it is out of the question to say that the text portrays what happened long ago, how it was thought to have been back then. First, there are at least two different stories about it. Second, the widespread evil alleged as cause of the Flood is not narrated. Third, evil is attributed to humankind after the Flood without, according to the text, so much as a day having passed in which such evil might have occurred. *Two different stories:* (1) the animals differ in quality (clean and unclean or undifferentiated) and in number (7 and 2 or 2 of all); (2) the blocks of time are different (40s and 7s or 150s); (3) the origin of the waters is different (from above or from above and below [7:11–12; 8:2]). *Evil before:* the wickedness of humankind is described as great (6:5) and the earth as corrupt and filled with violence (6:11); no corresponding state of affairs is narrated previously—Adam and Eve, Cain, Lamech, and company hardly fill the earth with violence. *Evil after:* God has no sooner smelled the pleasing odor of the sacrifice than humankind is pronounced evil (8:21); nested within God's blessing of Noah and his sons, there is fear and dread, the assumption of murder and capital punishment (9:2–6). The text deals with a situation Israel's theologians knew from their present experience; it is not a report of how things were thought to have happened back then.

The tower of Babel story (Gen 11:1–9) cannot be understood as portraying how it was thought to have been back then. First, "the earth had one language and the same words"

(11:1). In the previous chapter, however, the descendants of Noah's sons are carefully placed over the known earth, each with their own languages (see 10:5, 20, 31). Second, while the present text has only one story, it is complex and shows clear evidence of there having once been two versions (see vv. 5 and 7; also confusion of language and scattering abroad).

The conclusion is clear. These early stories in Genesis did not tell Israel and do not tell us how it was back then at the beginning, or even how it was thought to have been back then at the beginning. That leaves us with the very big question: why tell them at all? What did they mean? What do they mean? We begin by realizing that these stories of early times plumb the depths of human experience and explore the reality of human living in relationship with God, as it is now and always has been. Once we have realized this, the possibilities for interpretation are many—too many, alas, to be detailed here.

As is the case for all literature, while comparative study can be very helpful, the meaning of a text has to come from that text itself. In the case of these biblical texts, while the comparative study of other texts can be very helpful, the meaning of the biblical texts has to come from the biblical texts themselves. Awareness of Mesopotamian myth, for example, is extremely valuable; at the same time, what we believe these biblical texts mean has to emerge from our study of these biblical texts.

1. Multiple Portrayals of Creation
(Various Biblical Books)

Creation requires poetry. The smartest minds are overwhelmed by the facts and figures of its physics. Whether on the scale of galaxies or quarks, it is mind-blowing. When prose won't do, we turn to poetry.

When we look at our universe, the possibility that it just happened cannot be denied, even if the odds are incredibly slim. The possibility that it was created somehow cannot be denied either, even if that seems plainly incredible. When we say *created*, we say it all; the "somehow" is of minimum moment. But the Bible is marvelous on the "somehow."

There is God and the fashion industry:
> *You set the earth on its foundations...*
> > *you cover it with the deep as with a garment*
> > *(Ps 104:5);*

or God and the agricultural and catering industries:
> *You cause the grass to grow for the cattle,*
> > *and plants for people to use*
> *to bring forth food from the earth,*
> > *and wine to gladden the human heart*
> > *(Ps 104:14–15);*

and the God of night and day:
> *You make darkness, and it is night,*
> > *when all the animals of the forest come creeping*
> > *out....*
> *When the sun rises, they withdraw*
> > *and lie down in their dens.*
> *People go out to their work*
> > *and to their labor until the evening.*
> > *(Ps 104:20–23)*

Wisdom gets a kick out of creation, with delight and joy:
> *When he established the heavens, I was there,*
> > *when he drew a circle on the face of the deep,...*
> *when he marked out the foundation of the earth,*
> > *then I was beside him, like a master worker*
> *and I was daily his delight,*
> > *rejoicing before him always,*

> *rejoicing in his inhabited world*
> > *and delighting in the human race (Prov 8:27–31).*

Humans and the heavens themselves gasp in wonder:
> *When I look at your heavens, the work of your fingers*
> > *the moon and the stars that you have established;*
> *what are human beings that you are mindful of them,*
> > *mortals that you care for them? (Ps 8:3–4)*

and

> *Where were you when I laid the foundation of the*
> > *earth?...*
> *when the morning stars sang together*
> *and all the heavenly beings shouted for joy?*
> > *(Job 38:4, 7)*

There is the birth-giving, maternal image of God:
> *Or who shut in the sea with doors*
> > *when it burst out from the womb?—*
> *when I made the clouds its garment,*
> > *and thick darkness its swaddling band?*
> > *(Job 38:8–9)*

There is the power and violence of God too. Creation is not always calm and stately:
> *By his power he stilled the Sea;*
> > *by his understanding he struck down Rahab.*
> *By his wind the heavens were made fair;*
> > *his hand pierced the fleeing serpent*
> > *(Job 26:12–13);*

and

> *You divided the sea by your might;*
> > *you broke the heads of the dragons in the waters.*
> *You crushed the heads of Leviathan;*
> > *you gave him as food for the creatures of the*
> > *wilderness (Ps 74:13–14).*

For many people, all the Bible has to say about creation is found in Genesis 1. When they read more widely, they are in for a surprise.

2. Image of an Ideal World (Gen 1)

Genesis 1:1—2:4a is a marvelous text about the creative power of God: "In the beginning when God created the heavens and the earth...." For simple majesty, it is hard to beat. The body of the text is straightforward and clear, highly repetitive as it drives home its message: God did it all with sovereign power and unchallenged supremacy.

What is rather surprising, then, is that at the start and near the end are passages that are puzzling. At the start: did God create the "formless void" or was it already there and what was the situation pictured anyway? Near the end, "Let us make humankind in our image": what is this plural doing here for God? Despite the best of biblical scholarship, we can't answer these questions, so there is not much point in asking them.

The body of the text is superb. The rhythmic pattern rolls through the days, evening and morning, one through six. All eight works find their place; in fact, everything finds its place. Night and day were set up; "above" and "below" were separated by sky; earth and sea were established; on the earth, plants and trees flourished. The heavenly lights filled the sky; the fish teemed in the waters; the birds flew in the air above; animals roamed the earth; humans came on the scene to crown it all, in the image and likeness of God. Finally, God rested (as if on the Sabbath).

Everything is in perfect order. God is in perfect control. Alas, it is all too good to be true. Perhaps that is the point. It is majestically abstract, with no details to disturb its completeness. There are no emotions as in Proverbs 8, no valleys and streams as in Psalm 104, no mysteries as in Job 38, and certainly no combat as in Psalm 74. Everything is peaceful and perfect; everything is in its place.

Is it waiting for us humans to do our thing and mess it up? In what is to come, after transgression in the Garden, Cain will kill Abel, Lamech will boast of killing to avenge a wound, God will describe the earth as corrupt and filled with violence. A cynic might shrug and ask: what else is new? Genesis 1 insists that such is not the way it had to be. If the measures advocated by Deuteronomy were fully implemented, that is not the way it would be either.

According to Deuteronomy, all Israel was commanded to confess its belief in God three times a day: "YHWH is our God, YHWH alone" (Deut 6:4–9). All Israel's worship was centered on Jerusalem (Deut 12:5–7). All Israel's week was focused on the Sabbath (Deut 5:12–15). All Israel was guided by wise law (Deut 4:6–8). All Israel was the object of God's love (Deut 10:14–15). For all Israel—if only it feared the Lord its God, walked in all his ways, kept his commandments and his decrees (Deut 10:12–13)—everything would be in perfect order and God would be in perfect control. It would be a perfect world.

Israel had more than enough images of God's creative activity. Genesis 1 is unlike any of them. Did Genesis 1 celebrate the supremacy of God's sovereign power and wisdom? Did Genesis 1 portray an image of the ideal believed desirable within the world Israel's theologians believed God had created? Was Genesis 1 a portrayal of the potential excellence of God's creation, an ideal open to be realized? Was its portrayal of unparalleled order placed at the beginning in marked contrast to the portrayal of the subsequent disorder brought about by human activity? Could the image have been proclaimed with a view to bringing about God's ideal? Might a portrayal of the past have imaged an ideal for the future?

Genesis 1 may have been, and may still be, a faith statement about the image of the ideal understood to be latent in the world God was believed to have created. What in the text follows this image of the ideal, then, concerns the real world of Israel's experience. We cannot claim to be certain about what ancient authors might have meant. We can certainly claim the right for ourselves to read Genesis 1 in this way.

3. The Garden (Gen 2—3)

We all know about the beginning of Genesis. It is where Adam and Eve were created in a labor-free paradise, with the next chapter about how their disobedience and sin transformed God's beautiful world into the violent world we know—a fall from original grace because of original sin. Well, let's have a look at the biblical text. It may turn out to be about the ideal working world made for us by God (2:4b–25) and the reality of the less-than-ideal world we live in, with its inequality and oppression, made for us by ourselves.

"For the Lord God had not caused it to rain upon the earth, and there was no one to till the ground" (2:5). So that's why the earth was barren; no water and no worker. But what a surprise that the text takes for granted that from the very outset humans would work the earth. Later we were put in the garden "to till it and keep it" (2:15), but from the beginning verse 5 takes work for granted.

The story of Genesis 2—3 is not as simple as most of us have been brought up to believe. We think of one tree in the middle of the garden, the tree of the knowledge of good and evil. But according to 2:9, there were two trees "in the middle of the garden." The serpent and the woman talked about "the tree that is in the middle of the garden" (3:3). Fortunately, God was quite specific about which tree was forbidden: you shall not eat of "the tree of the knowledge of good and evil" (2:17). But then that's a surprise. For if they "may freely eat of every tree of the garden" (2:16), they are allowed to eat of the tree of life. I did say it wasn't simple. It's a complex text that invites us to think!

The God of this biblical text is not a potter—more of an earthmover. Potters form things, but they use clay. The text has God form everything, but God uses "the dust of the ground" (2:7) or just "the ground" (2:19). No potter would be so foolish. Hebrew has a word for clay, as English does. There are texts that say we were made out of clay, but not Genesis 2.

"Out of the ground the Lord God formed every animal...and every bird" (2:19). The image is of a hard-working God—unquestionably grubby and sweaty. God was doing all this for our good. "It is not good that the man should be alone" (2:18). The text has God making all the animals and birds and checking them with the man. God's commitment to human well-being is not taken lightly.

"Woman" rates a higher origin than the birds, the animals, and the man. Rather than being shaped from the ground or the dust, she is shaped from a human flank or rib. She is the counterpart of man (support and mirror image, 2:18). With woman, the man is no longer alone; the community of humankind is complete. The story has a final surprise: the man leaves mummy and daddy and clings to his wife (2:24). I'd have bet the family farm it would be the other way around.

We should not be surprised that in Genesis 3 the snake speaks. In such stories, animals have their say. The snake is a creature, the most crafty. The snake could easily stand for the seductive aspects of our lives that take us away from the intangible spirit within us, except that the seductive in life usually turns out to be illusion and wrong—and the snake turns out to be right.

That's the first surprise in this story: the snake is right and God is wrong. The snake says: "You will not die" (3:4).

They do not die. The snake says: "Your eyes will be opened" (3:5). Their eyes are opened (3:7). The snake says: "You will be like God, knowing good and evil" (3:5). They become like God, knowing good and evil (3:22). God had said: "In the day that you eat of it you shall die" (2:17). They ate of it; they did not die that day. It is not a simple story.

A second surprise for most of us is the role of the woman, portrayed as far wiser and more responsible than the man. Ignoring the snake's temptation, the story has the woman see that the tree is "good for food," "a delight to the eyes," and "to be desired to make one wise." The text does not suggest that these observations are illusory. They concern nourishment, beauty, and insight. The story has the woman observe and reflect—then she eats. She gives to her husband—he eats. The text does not claim one moment of reflection for him. It is not a simple story.

Her husband was "with her." What manner of man, having had the command directly from God, could be beside the woman during her exchange with the snake and not say a word? When she is looking at the tree and reflecting on its nutritional, aesthetic, and prudential values, the man with her is not given a word to say! What experience does this text distill? There is something strange and surprising here. It is a highly complex story.

Given the long tradition that this text reports a change in the quality of life for all human beings to come, it is surprising that the only reference to offspring is the innocuous one of the enmity of humans for snakes (3:15). Promises to the ancestors specify descendants, even in perpetuity. Promises and threats to kings tend to specify descendants and dynasties. There is nothing of that here. Oddly enough, after Genesis 5:5 Adam does not rate another mention in the Hebrew scriptures (beyond 1 Chron 1:1); the Greek deutero-canonical books have Tobit 8:6 and Sirach 40:1; 49:16.

None suggests Adam's responsibility for the human condition. Surprise! Eve, and the figures to come (Cain and Abel, Lamech and Noah), don't get a mention in the rest of the Hebrew Bible either—except for Noah in Isaiah 54:9.

Final surprise: the man is driven out of the garden lest "he might reach out his hand and take also from the tree of life, and eat, and live forever" (3:22). What is this text all about? Was the woman part of this version? The beginning of wisdom is to know what we do not know. This is unquestionably a story of sin, of limit transgressed, of prohibition violated; beyond this, nothing is unquestionable.

4. The Flood (Gen 6:5—9:17)

Beyond serious doubt, there are two relatively complete accounts of the Flood in Genesis 6:5—9:17. Naturally, we can smooth out passages here and there; the compilers who put the combined text together were competent operators. The reality of two relatively complete accounts, however, cannot be avoided. Because two names are used for God, *YHWH* (personal name) and *elohim* (common noun), one in each account, it is simple to designate the two as the *YHWH*-account and the *elohim*-account. The high quality of their theology is remarkable; as remarkable are the theological differences between them.

To summarize swiftly, the principal differences between the two are: the names for God; the blocks of time; the nature and number of the animals; the origins of the floodwaters.

In the *YHWH*-account, (1) the blocks of time are counted mainly as seven days and forty days; (2) the animals are both clean and unclean, seven clean and two unclean (probably pairs), described as "the male and its mate"; (3) the origin of the floodwaters is from above ("the rain").

In the *elohim*-account, (1) the blocks of time are counted mainly as 150 days; (2) the animals are undifferentiated as to ritual cleanliness ("two of every kind"), described as "male and female"; (3) the origin of the floodwaters is both from above ("the windows of the heavens") and from below ("the fountains of the great deep").

The *YHWH*-account begins with a real shocker. "The Lord saw that the wickedness of humankind was great in the earth and that every inclination of the thoughts of their hearts was only evil continually" (6:5). Even after all the horrors of the last century or so, we could hardly put it more bluntly and brutally. That the wickedness of humankind has been great is beyond dispute; history leaves no doubt. The "only evil continually" may be considered harsh, but is certainly true where large blocks of human activity have been concerned. God is not portrayed as angry, but as "sorry" and "grieved." So God concludes: I am sorry that I made them; I will wipe out the lot. In the *YHWH*-account, it is only at this point, as it were the exception that will keep humankind alive, that Noah gets a mention as finding favor in God's sight (6:8).

To the contrary, the *elohim*-account begins with a couple of verses about Noah as blameless and righteous and walking with God. It even mentions his sons (6:9–10). Then comes the judgment on the world, but—surprisingly— humans do not rate a specific mention. Instead of singling out humankind, the focus is on "the earth" as corrupt and filled with violence, because "all flesh" (which, of course, includes humankind) had corrupted its ways on the earth. Only then does the narrator have God tell Noah that there is going to be a flood to destroy "all flesh." This phrase, "all flesh," which occurs twelve times between Genesis 6:12 and 9:17 (all in the *elohim*-account), does not occur at all in Genesis 1 (or elsewhere in Genesis). It looks as if this account had a life all of its own; no wonder it is complete. And, in this *elohim*-account, God's opening speech ends with the covenant to be made with Noah (6:18), and the intention of preserving in the ark Noah's wife and children and representatives of the whole animal world.

These are introductory avenues leading to two very different theologies. In the first, the emphasis is entirely on the human race, seen as thoroughly evil. Noah is mentioned at the end as "finding favor in the sight of the Lord." In the text we have, nothing is said about any ark or any lifesaving; we can assume something was there in the original *YHWH*-account (see 7:1). In the second, Noah's goodness is to the fore, the human race is lost sight of in the generic "all flesh," and a covenant and the ark are explicit lifesavers.

The necessary combination of the two accounts has been very competently done. At the beginning, the horror of human evil is to the fore; the goodness of Noah is central; the announcement of the flood to come ends with the promise of salvation. In the *YHWH*-account, what happens at the end is not prepared for in any way. The mention that Noah "found favor" (6:8) is a pointer to survival to come; nothing hints at what actually is to come. What happens is a total reversal on the part of God (8:21–22). In the *elohim*-account, the ark, the covenant, and those in it prepare for what is to follow. It is not to be a total reversal on the part of God, but a change in God's plans. The combined account does not shrink from the horror of human reality. The combined account emphasizes that life will go on.

In any telling of a flood story, the middle is relatively predictable. The floodwaters arrive; all aboard. The ark floats; the rest drown. The floodwaters subside; all ashore.

It is the ending of the Flood story that is a real surprise and that as biblical texts go is a brilliant piece of the profoundest theology. Both stories are surprisingly unpredictable.

The *YHWH*-account comes first. God is portrayed alone ("said in his heart"), completely changing God's mind.

For the same reason that God sent the Flood in the first place (because of human wickedness), for that same reason God will never do it again. The reason is given in almost the same words as it was at the beginning: "for the inclination of the human heart is evil from youth" (8:21). At the beginning, it was harsher: "every inclination," "only evil," and "continually" (6:5). So at the end the verdict is softened a little, but the softening is slight. More surprising even than God's change of mind is the reality that in the portrayal there is absolutely no evidence to support God's verdict. Noah and his crew are just off the ark. All they have done is offer a sacrifice; its odor was pleasing to God. The evidence that "the inclination of the human heart is evil from youth" (8:21) does not come from the story. It can come from Israel's experience of human living over the centuries. If so, the narrative is not about how things were back then, but about how things have always been, *from* the very beginning until now—as it was in the beginning, is now, and always was.

The *elohim*-account comes next (9:1–17) and is just as surprising. God talks to Noah and his sons, so down on earth. Under the new dispensation, the world they are to repeople will have "fear and dread" resting on every animal (9:2) and, at the human level, murder and capital punishment (9:6). The surprise: with this less-than-perfect world, God is portrayed making an unconditional and everlasting covenant never again to destroy the earth with a flood (9:8–17).

Putting the two accounts together helps to lessen God's unpredictability. The human wickedness of 6:5 and 8:21 is combined with the change of divine dispensation for the world. Unquestionably, God is portrayed as having come to terms with a less-than-perfect world. The claim of a new humanity starting afresh here is old nonsense that should be encouraged to disappear. Human existence is not threatened by divine holiness. This is not a reflection on "back then"; it is a faith claim for "right now."

As astounding as anything else is the realization that Israel has exploited universal mythology for its own quite particular theological purposes. Over the last century or two, biblical scholarship has become more and more aware of Israel's immersion in the ancient Near Eastern mythology of its time. In such mythology, as in almost all mythologies, the theme of a flood bulks large. In the ancient Near East, it was used as a narrative about the past in a polytheistic setting where one god can disagree with another. Israel's theologians have used it as a narrative relating to present experience and situated in a monotheistic setting, where with only one God, God must change God's mind. Astounding indeed!

Here, in a double tradition, the All-holy is committed to the continued existence of the less-than-perfect—to us. It is the most profound theology, a theology of the human relationship with God. God is committed to us, less than perfect though we are. We are loved, sinners though we are. Right from the beginnings!

REFLECTIVE MOMENTS
FOR PART ONE

What a relief that the Bible was not trying to teach us all about creation; it doesn't have to be primitive and wrong after all. Genesis 1 could certainly be a stately portrayal of creation. What a fascinating idea that it might also be an image of an ideal world, properly ordered, fostering life, peace, and prosperity. Not the mechanics of a past creation but possibly the portrayal of an ideal of wholeness for a future world.

Language that God *created* the world or the universe can perhaps suggest to some a detailed "nuts and bolts" picture of divine creative activity. Am I more comfortable with language like God *envisioned* the world or the universe—taking for granted that God did whatever was needed to bring it about? Does my faith allow me to imagine God envisioning the vastness of our universe and wanting a race of humans—"us"— out there on the minuteness of a planet "earth"?

※

How comfortable am I with the idea that our world has always been much the way it is? Am I a bit ashamed to associate the world I know with the creative activity of God? Does this mean that I am not too comfortable accepting that God loves me the way I am? Do I give up on trying to improve myself or our world? Where do I fit Jesus into all this?

※

I'd always thought of the Garden story as an account of where sin came from and of the Flood as an angry God's response to human sin. The Flood story as portraying a change of heart, a change in God, a tolerant God really rejoices me. The Garden story as a reflection of our ability to turn a blind eye to what we know as right does not surprise me half as much.

Reflective Activity

Listen to a piece of music that evokes some of the images and feelings you have about the Garden and Flood stories. What do you become aware of in the experience of being present to the music?

PART TWO:
Faith, Faithlessness, and Fear

ABRAHAM AND JACOB

Introduction

In days gone by, the ancestors of Israel were firmly associated with the promise of heirs and land (see Walter Brueggemann, *Genesis* [1982], 109–110). The land of Israel was referred to as the "promised land"; the Book of Joshua was associated with the five books that preceded it (to form a Hexateuch), because it was felt that the fulfillment of what had been promised had to have been narrated.

However, if texts such as Genesis 17 (from around the time of Israel's exile) and Genesis 15 (likely to be late) are left aside, minimal attention is given to the promise of a specific heir or of specific land in the other Abraham traditions. Neither promise is central to the Jacob cycle. Where an heir is concerned, Jacob is the forerunner for "cheaper by the dozen"; he has eleven sons and a daughter. Benjamin came later. Land was hardly a concern. Jacob occupied land at Succoth, east of the Jordan and south of the Jabbok (Gen 33:17), and bought land at Shechem (33:18); later, he is reported to have journeyed south, through Bethel (where he never settled), to a place "beyond the tower of Eder" (a location unknown to us).

The Abraham cycle is clearly a combination of various traditions with its meaning well concealed. The Jacob cycle is more unified, but its meaning is just as veiled. The indicators are not there to tell us how ancient Israel understood its traditions about these two—apart from Genesis 15 and 17 for Abraham. We are entitled to explore how we understand them for ourselves.

For Abraham, it is clear that he is portrayed trusting God in his response to God's call (Gen 12) and in his response regarding the sacrifice or binding of Isaac (22). In between, it is fairly clear that despite God's promise to make him "a great nation," he is portrayed not trusting this promise when in Egypt (12:10–20), not trusting it when Sarah is barren (16), and not trusting it again when it comes to choosing between Sarah's surrogate son (Hagar's Ishmael) and the son God had given Sarah (21). Small wonder Genesis 22 is so demanding.

For Jacob, it is clear that early in the Jacob cycle he fled from Esau in fear for his life and that late in the cycle returning to Canaan he feared for his life again when faced with meeting Esau. There is rift and there is healing. It may not be unimportant, but for the moment its importance may elude us.

Allowing for the likelihood that Genesis 27 is a late composition, conjectures associated with the time of exile are clearly possible; as things stand at present, they cannot be confirmed. Given the memory of Edomite hostility around the fall of Jerusalem ("Tear it down!" [Ps 137:7–9]), it is not impossible that Jacob's departure from a hostile Esau and his return to build the nation of Israel could have been seen to reflect later Israel's departure into exile, leaving behind a hostile Edom. In the tradition, Jacob's return led to a flourishing nation; Israel, on its return from exile, may have hoped for the same. Is it thinkable that, to find a glimmer of life and hope in the midst of the catastrophe of exile, an earlier tradition ("Two *nations* are in your womb...the elder shall serve the younger" [Gen 25:23]) should have been resurrected and reshaped?

Whatever such conjectures, readers will be aware that once again the woman's choice prevails (Eve, Sarah, Rebekah). What archetypal drive was at work in ancient Israel?

We will not explore the Lot and Esau material here or the texts relating to Ishmael. One aspect, however, is worth our noting. All three are portrayed as family and all three end up being distanced from Israel. They are family: Lot is Abraham's nephew; Ishmael is Abraham's son; Esau is Jacob's brother. Lot and Esau end up on the far side of the Jordan: Lot as ancestor of the Moabites and Ammonites, and Esau as ancestor of the Edomites. Ishmael is not given a specific location in the texts, but we find the Ishmaelites flourishing to the south of Israel. What these moves mean we do not exactly know; what we do know is that they must have been somehow significant.

5. The Journey: Abraham's First Faith (Gen 12)

Many think of the Jews as the "chosen people" and are left wondering whether that means some people miss out. The beginning of the story of Abraham is a wonderfully warming one. In the call of Abraham, which is the beginning of the Jewish people (from the point of view of biblical text), all of us are in view. "In you all the families of the earth shall be blessed" (Gen 12:3). God's relationship with Abraham is not just for the descendants of Abraham; it is to bring blessing to all the families of the earth.

Whatever else this means, it has to mean a faith in Israel that God's desire for all the families of the earth is for them to be in right relationship with God, on good terms with God, to be blessed. Not bad for a start and not bad for the destiny of Israel.

The same commitment, in identical words, is made to Jacob (Gen 28:14). With a minor change in language, it is repeated about Abraham, in connection with intercession for sinners (18:18). With a further minor change in language, it is repeated again to Abraham after the story of the sacrifice of Isaac, of Isaac's binding (22:18) and, with this language, to Isaac (26:4). Its spirit is present in Isaiah 19:24–25 (if you haven't read this text, stop right here; find a Bible and read it). Its letter is alive for Saint Paul as part of the Christian good news (Gal 3:8). The minor changes within stereotypical language, indicating three levels where the concern endured, and the occurrences in Isaiah and Paul show that it covers a wide sweep of scripture. It signals to us faith in a God whose longing is for blessing for the whole human race.

This bit of good news opens the chapter. It is the conclusion of a speech given to God that has remarkable theological density. Abraham is told to leave his country and follow God's call. His country is spelled out in three terms: "your country...your kindred...your father's house." All three spell out what is familiar to him. He is to follow God's call and go "to the land that I will show you" (12:1). No more than that; no destination, no itinerary, simply "the land that I will show you"—the unfamiliar.

Two further elements follow in the promise put on God's lips: "I will make of you a great nation" and "I will bless you...you will be a blessing" (12:2). In the traditions to follow, it is this promise to make of Abraham a great nation that he will be portrayed as failing to trust. Finally, in calling for the sacrifice of Isaac's life, God will be portrayed as requiring a trust of Abraham that puts the whole issue of descendants, nation, and blessing at risk.

Meantime, this opening passage has Abraham do what he has been commanded to do. He went, "as the Lord had told him." On arrival in Canaan, Abraham (named Abram at this point in the text) journeyed to Shechem and built an altar there (12:6–7), then on to a spot between Bethel and Ai and built an altar there (12:8), and finally to Hebron where he settled and built an altar to the Lord (13:18).

An observant reader realizes at once that to reach this destination at Hebron we have skipped Abraham's sojourn in Egypt and his separation from his nephew Lot. An observant reader will also have realized that, despite the altars built, Abraham has not been promised this land. In 12:7, the land is promised to his offspring; there is no mention before 13:14–17 of God's giving the land to Abraham. In fact, the gift in 13:14–17 is problematic, because Abraham has just given Lot his free choice and Lot has chosen the Jordan valley (13:10–11). It is not a long-term problem, since Lot will be out of there in a few chapters' time (with the destruction of Sodom and Gomorrah), but still, in the short term, some narrator-theologian had no right to have God offer it as a gift to Abraham. Of course, if a storyteller had wanted to tell a version of the narrative using the Abraham traditions exclusively (without incorporating the Lot traditions), a most appropriate ending to conclude the story of Abraham's migration, following immediately on 12:8, would have been God's gift of the land to Abraham and Abraham's settling in Hebron (text now located in 13:14–18, where in v. 14a it has a little clause accommodating Lot).

There is no question of the portrayal of Abraham's faith in his leaving all that was familiar in response to God's call. As observant readers, however, we will note that the promise of an heir is not explicit in its own right; it is contained in the promise to make of him "a great nation" and the first mention of a promise of the land is in reference to Abraham's descendants (12:7; at Shechem, later Jacob's territory).

6. The Doubts: Abraham's Failed Faith
(Gen 12, 16, 21)

Abraham comes out badly in Genesis 12:10–20. Whatever of Sarah's beauty or Abraham's resourcefulness, he is portrayed as an exploitative liar with a prejudice against foreigners—and no evidence of trust in God. Yet he is our ancestor in faith; there is hope for us. Perhaps there was hope also for Israel.

If Abraham is to be made "a great nation" (12:2), he will not die in Egypt. Yet in the little story, Abraham is portrayed knowing Sarah is a beautiful woman and fearing the Egyptians will recognize her as his wife and kill him because he is her husband; so he tells her, "Say you are my sister (keeping quiet about her position as his wife), so that it may go well with me because of you" (12:13; cf. vv. 12, 18). As a result, Sarah was taken into Pharaoh's harem and "for her sake" Pharaoh dealt well with Abraham. In the story, Abraham misjudges the Egyptians, does not put his trust in God, and does put his wife at risk to save his skin. Not nice.

With major variations, of course, the motif occurs twice more (for Abraham and Sarah with Abimelech at Gerar [Gen 20:1–18] and for Isaac and Rebekah with Abimelech again at Gerar [26:6–11]). The repeated telling points to an importance for the ancient narrators that is as yet not wholly clear to us.

Sarah recognizes her sterility ("the Lord has prevented me from bearing children") and suggests that Abraham have intercourse with her Egyptian maid and so bear children for her ("it may be that I shall obtain children by her"). Instead of trusting his God (to whom, by the way, the storyteller has Sarah attribute her barrenness [16:2]), Abraham obeys Sarah and Hagar becomes pregnant by Abraham and contemptuous of Sarah whose subsequent brutality to Hagar makes it an ugly story. The story as it is given in the biblical text has two women being beastly to each other, one using power conceded her by a weak and ineffectual male to make life intolerable for the other. The ugliness of this can distract readers from the reality that Abraham did not trust God to provide his heir from whom might come the great nation.

There is much to be said about Hagar, her resourcefulness and survival in Genesis 16, her victim status in Genesis 21. But our focus here is on Abraham.

Sarah is portrayed as exultant at the birth of her child, Isaac, promised by God (18:10–14) and given by God in due time (21:1–2, 6). She is also portrayed as telling Abraham to get rid of Hagar and Ishmael, "for the son of this slave woman shall not inherit along with my son Isaac" (21:10). Not nice at all.

Is it fair to Abraham to say that he failed for a third time to trust God because of his obedience to Sarah in sending away Hagar and Ishmael (21:10–11)? The two-verse divine speech in 21:12–13 exonerates Abraham from such failure; the fact that the matter was "very distressing" suggests that perhaps he did not trust until given God's explicit assurance; his subsequent silence about the assurance is troubling. Abraham has been reassured by God that Ishmael will survive. The text does not have him say a word to Hagar about it; worse, she clearly does not know (v. 16).

The decision has been made by Sarah (as it will be in the next generation by Rebekah) and is backed by God. "Whatever Sarah says to you, do as she tells you" (21:12). The decision is not Abraham's; the initiative is not God's. Both initiative and decision come from Sarah, the archetypal mother.

We do not know how these stories were handled by Israel's storytellers; we only have the texts from which the storytelling presumably was launched. As mentioned earlier, we have the right to ask ourselves what meaning we can make of the texts before us, difficult though that may sometimes be.

The story of Genesis 21 is strange. It prepares the way for Genesis 22, the sacrifice of Isaac. Sarah demands of Abraham in Genesis 21 what God demands of Abraham in Genesis 22—the loss of a son. Genesis 22 is surely exploring the depths of the human experience of God.

7. Unbelievable Faith at Unbelievable Cost: Abraham's Final Faith (Gen 22)

This is a story that does not yield meaning easily. As an event, it would have been appalling. For Abraham: whose voice did I think I was hearing? For Isaac: what did my father think he was doing? For us, the task is to make meaning of the story. Readers must find that meaning for themselves. Some call this one of the Bible's best stories, others one of the Bible's worst. All we can do is look at it and wonder what emerges from it for us.

A key to the meaning I make of it is in the emphasis on trust: "God himself will provide," "the Lord will provide," and "on the mount of the Lord it shall be provided" (22:8, 14a, b). For me, it is a story of basic trust—but a fearful story. In its present place in the text, it is Abraham's final act of trusting faith after the preceding failures. If Abraham trusts in God's promise, he believes that God will not do anything that might endanger that promise. Somehow, Israel's experience of God is in this story. Is ours?

The text opens with the statement that "God tested Abraham." A test can tell God something about Abraham or something about God. A test can tell Abraham something about God or something about Abraham. What does this test tell us? The end of the angel's second call identifies the test as obedience (22:18). There may be more to it than that.

The story begins with the identification of the victim and the naming of the task. The Hebrew has an explicit triple movement in the victim's identification (for some reason most translations do not reflect this): "your son, your only son whom you love, Isaac"—the relationship, the bond, finally the name. The triple movement echoes Abraham's call: leave your country, your kindred, and your father's house (Gen 12:1). Is this Israel's experience of God: leave the familiar and in the unknown find God? The task named ("offer him there as a burnt offering") is totally destructive for Abraham: his beloved only son and the whole promise of nation, name, and blessing (12:2).

The silence of the journey is broken only by the poignant exchange of father and son: father, father, my son, my son. Dialogue in Hebrew narrative does not normally spell out such relationships.

The text does not attempt any realism as to how Abraham managed to bind and lift his son. The actions flow ruthlessly and bluntly one after the other: the place, the altar, the wood, the binding, the placing, on top of the wood. The detail is excruciating: he reached out his hand—he took the knife—to kill his son.

The angel's first call stops the story (22:11–12); the second call essays an interpretation (22:15–18). "You have not withheld your son...You have obeyed my voice." How are we to interpret these added verses, this second call? Do they replace trust with obedience? I would hope not. Do they add obedience as a further element to be understood in Abraham's trust? It is possible.

The story is stripped very bare. There is no mention of Isaac's return with his father. Could a storyteller expect that of Isaac? Abraham lived at Beer-sheba (22:19). Did Isaac? There is no mention of Isaac afterward within the story. There is no mention of Sarah before or after. Is this a story of the aloneness of the human individual's encounter with life, with God? It would be easier if it were just a report of an event, but it almost certainly is not. What in it holds us bound? Could we trust? Do we trust?

In the Abraham cycle, this story is practically speaking the end. Genesis 23 is about Sarah's death and burial; Genesis 24 is about the quest for a wife for Isaac. In Genesis 25, Abraham is dead (v. 8). Is Genesis 22 tradition's final word on Abraham? In the end, Abraham had faith and trusted God.

As a story, Genesis 22 is mind-blowing. For me, it is as mystifying as the reality of Christ crucified—foolishness, folly, absurdity, or madness, but the core of Christian faith (see 1 Cor 1:23–25; "for God's foolishness is wiser than human wisdom, and God's weakness is stronger than human strength"). On occasion in the Older Testament and throughout the whole Bible we find our minds are blown apart. It is the risk of faith. If we domesticate and tame our faith, it is our loss. Faith in God is a huge risk; we believe dangerously. So did Abraham.

8. Jacob's Sin: Rift with Esau (Gen 27)

Genesis 12—50 is about our ancestors in faith. Usually we tidy up the stories of our forebears. Not in Genesis. With our eyes open, there are some nasty surprises. The biggest surprise of all: God loved them. But then: their God loves us!

Neither Jacob nor his mother comes out of this story very nicely. We have to wonder why it was told, especially as there are strong grounds for seeing it as a late text. It is a story that is told rather than an event that is remembered. In the narrative, old Isaac preferred Esau, but Rebekah loved Jacob (25:28). Rebekah saw to it that she got her way, even if it cost her the presence of the son she loved. The text has

Esau adequately sum up his brother: is he not rightly named Jacob? He has cheated me twice (27:36).

It would be a storyteller's delight. The son is pliant and fearful: what if I bring a curse on myself? (27:12). The tough-minded, scheming mother is unafraid: let your curse be on me, my son (27:13). Rebekah calls the shots: "now therefore, my son, obey my word as I command you" (27:8). She decides on the two kids from the family flock; she cooks up the savory food; she takes Esau's clothes so Jacob would smell right; she puts the pelts on him so he'd feel right. Jacob is the pliant and fearful one, worried that he might be found out. The scene with the old Isaac is brilliant. How did you find the game so quickly, son? Your God granted me success, Dad. The old man's doubts are not so easily allayed. Sounds like Jacob; feels like Esau. After the food and the wine, one more test: the smell is right (27:27).

Jacob clears out with the blessing. Esau comes in with the game Isaac had asked for. The scene is heartbreaking. Old Isaac trembles violently: who gave me the food and got my blessing? (27:33). Esau's grief is bitter and loud; the blessing that is left for him is miserly.

Esau hates Jacob; he'll kill him (27:41). So Rebekah, who loved her Jacob, has now lost both sons; Esau can be assumed to hate her and Jacob needs to absent himself to save his skin. The text doesn't mention Esau's feelings toward his mother, although a storyteller could have; the text doesn't need to. An audience can be assumed to recognize that Esau would have been smart enough to know his mother's role in Jacob's deceit; Jacob didn't have the nerve to pull it off for himself. Rebekah tells Jacob to leave town. Esau planned his marriages to suit his father—no word of Esau's concern for his mother (28:8–9). She lost them both.

The surprising aspect of this story is that it is there, that it is told. It would have to be a gem in the storyteller's repertoire. But how did it get into the canon of Israel's sacred scripture? It sorts out bloodlines, with Jacob marrying and raising his family back in Uncle Laban's territory and Esau adding Ishmael's daughter to his wives. Esau's territory will be in the south, around Mount Seir, east of the Dead Sea. Jacob will settle more to the north, around Succoth and Shechem, either side of the Jordan. But these issues of genealogy and land, important as they may be in a broader context, are peripheral to the story here.

Why tell such a story? Abraham may have been the first ancestral figure for Israel. Jacob was the greatest. He gave his name, Jacob/Israel, to the nation. His sons were the forebears of its tribes. The figure in Israel's great credo, "a wandering Aramean was my ancestor" (Deut 26:5), is Jacob. Why is so great a figure celebrated as a mother's boy, a timid lad, and a two-timing cheat?

Later, Jacob's name came to be associated with the kingdom of northern Israel, more powerful and more significant than Judah to the south. In 722, the northern kingdom came to a crushing end at the hands of the Assyrians. As the biblical text stands, this story and Genesis 24 are needed to bring Jacob into the family of Abraham. Might this story of a rather-less-than-admirable Jacob perhaps have resonated with traces of a superior attitude on the part of surviving Judah toward its failed northern neighbor?

The rift with Esau is evident. In fear of his life, Jacob takes flight. He will not meet Esau again until almost the end of the Jacob cycle. Why was the story told? Appeal to tradition answers nothing. Why the tradition? We can say this for ourselves today: if God's love rested on an unprincipled sinner of this caliber, God's love can surely rest on us. Did Israel entertain the same thought?

9. Jacob's Healing: Reconciliation with Esau (Gen 32)

Along with Genesis 22, this has to rate as one of the Bible's great stories exploring the human encounter alone with God, in Jacob's case before he encounters his brother Esau.

Jacob is coming home, after a long stay abroad. Esau is coming to meet him, with four hundred men—which left Jacob "greatly afraid and distressed." Jacob took his two wives, his two maids, his eleven children, and all that he had across the stream. The direction does not matter. What matters is that Jacob was left alone (32:24–25).

With him, Jacob brought a weighty burden of baggage on his conscience. According to Esau, Jacob had stolen his birthright (27:36; cf. 25:29–34). According to the text, he aided and abetted his mother in cheating Esau out of the eldest son's blessing (27:1–45). The rights and wrongs of his dealings with his Uncle Laban are debatable. The text preserves a tradition of Jacob's taking the opportunity while Laban was away shearing to clear out with his wives and all his possessions; the situation was such that Laban took after him in hot pursuit with the ancient Near Eastern equivalent of a posse (31:23). They settled for what might be called a nonaggression pact (31:51–54). All this lay behind Jacob; in front of him was Esau, whom Jacob feared might kill him (32:11).

In these circumstances, Jacob was on his own, at the river, and "a man wrestled with him until daybreak" (32:24). Nothing is said in the text about why the wrestling took place. In some stories, the guardian of the ford had to be vanquished in order to cross over. In some circumstances, people have to confront their consciences in order to move beyond their past.

The strangeness of the story is signaled from the start: they wrestled "until daybreak." Why until daybreak? The text leaves us with the question while it turns to the wrestling's dirty tricks. The opponent sees he can't win, so somehow he dislocates Jacob's hip. The text says nothing more but, given the exchange that follows, Jacob must have hung in there. When there is nothing else we can do, we can always hang on or hang in.

Daybreak becomes significant when the opponent says, "Let me go, for the day is breaking" (32:26). Only spirit beings need to disappear at dawn? Who is this "man"? Back at the start, the Hebrew text had called him "a man." Since then, in the Hebrew text, he has not been named, represented simply by the third-person masculine, "he." Now he claims he must disappear at dawn. Spirits and demons of the night disappear at dawn. Who is this man?

"Let me go," he says. States Jacob, "I will not let you go, unless you bless me" (32:26). Then he asks Jacob's name and changes it to Israel—and the reason he gives suggests his identity. "For you have striven with God and with men and have prevailed." The men could be Esau and Laban; the "man" could be God. Jacob asks for his opponent's name and isn't given it; instead he is given a blessing.

The end of the story leaves no doubt of the opponent's identity; it was God. "I have seen God face to face, and yet my life is preserved." The sun rose "upon him" as Jacob passed the place, limping. The struggle made him lame; the blessing gave him life. Christians will recall it being said: "unless a grain of wheat falls into the earth and dies, it remains just a single grain; but if it dies, it bears much fruit" (John 12:24). A surprising story, but oh how true.

In the struggle, Jacob was made lame, but somehow he was also healed ("the sun rose upon him"). He had met God face to face and his life was preserved. In the coming day, he

would meet Esau face to face and his life would be preserved. But why did this meeting matter enough to Israel to
tell the story?

REFLECTIVE MOMENTS
FOR PART TWO

Abraham is portrayed as promised rich blessing, as
obliged to go down to Egypt to escape famine, and as engag-
ing in less than salubrious behavior there. As he and Sarah are
ejected by the pharaoh, no less, a silent-movie caption would
be obliged to read: THE LIAR LEAVES. This is my ancestor.
Am I comforted, encouraged, or scandalized; or do all three
have a place in me? Jacob is portrayed as behaving just as
badly, pretty much from the outset of his story. His silent-
movie caption after Genesis 27 would be obliged to read: THE
CHEAT BOLTS. Yet, on the run, staying overnight at Bethel,
he is portrayed as promised rich blessing. These are my ancestors in faith; also involved is my God. Am I comforted,
encouraged, scandalized, or all three?

Alas, the women do no better. Sarah is portrayed as
brutal and demanding, Rebekah as scheming and manipulative. Am I comforted, encouraged, or scandalized?

In different ways, Lot, Ishmael, and Esau are distanced
from the ancestral figures. They are not demeaned, not
diminished, only distanced. Am I lost in admiration for
Israel's thinkers, or for the breadth of God's commitment, or
for faith's capacity to accommodate to political reality?

I had thought of Israel's stories of its ancestors (Abraham, Isaac, and Jacob; Sarah, Rebekah, and Rachel) as reflecting traditions of the people's origins in their distant past. Faith, faithlessness, and fear lend themselves to Israel's reflection on matters relevant to their present. How comfortable am I with that? How comfortable am I with the place of God in my own present?

Reflective Activity

What movies portray characters like Abraham, Sarah, Rebekah, Lot, Ishmael, or Esau? What responses did the characters in the films evoke in you?

PART THREE:
Immigrants and Survivors

LAND AND LIFE

Introduction

There is little doubt that the Book of Joshua, with its stories of Israel's "conquest of the promised land," has generated more resentment and controversy than any other part of the Bible. The problem is simple: how could God promise the land to Israel when the locals were already living there? The solution to the problem generated resentment and controversy in abundance, understandably. After all, with regard to the local inhabitants, the practical solution was: eliminate them.

Such resentment and controversy, understandable as it may be, is most unfair to the Book of Joshua for at least two reasons. First, there is a great deal more going on in it than this; and even the worst of this is restricted to a handful of verses, especially Joshua 10:28–40. Second, Israel was perfectly aware that it had not eliminated the locals; otherwise, why the prohibition against intermarriage with them and that sort of thing? Had the locals been wiped out, such prohibitions would have been unnecessary. Something else is running; we are, as yet, not precisely sure what.

The primary problems with the Book of Joshua are with the first half, 1—12. The second half is about the allocation of the land among the tribes and attracts little animosity. In the Book of Judges, on the other hand, it is the second half that is problematic. The first half is highly theological and attracts plenty of attention but minimal animosity. After the Samson stories, Judges 17—21 is seriously puzzling because much of it is so manifestly out of touch with Israel's reality. It will not be explored here.

Much has been made in the past of archaeology's success in demonstrating the veracity of the Book of Joshua. With more careful scrutiny and more accurate excavation, this boast has been replaced with an honest avowal that no clear picture has emerged—from excavation or from the Bible—that either sheds light on Israel's entry into the land or helps account for Israel's presence in the land. Recent discoveries of evidence for initially two to three hundred newly established unfortified highland villages, mainly in the hill country from southern Galilee to northern Negev, suggest a potentially early Israelite movement, with a gradual transformation from pastoral to agricultural life. It appears unrelated to any picture derived from the Joshua accounts. In turn, this may allow the Joshua accounts to be evaluated for their own worth and meaning.

(A) ISRAEL'S ENTRY INTO THE LAND OF CANAAN

10. Israel's Move into the Land (Josh 1—12)

Much is to be learned about the Bible from the Book of Joshua. It holds remnants of at least three views of how Israel came to occupy its land—and these three views are not necessarily compatible with one another, or with what may have actually happened. In one, Israel conquered the land, with God's help. According to a second, God handled the conquest of the land on Israel's behalf. In a third, Israel totally emptied the land of its inhabitants, men, women, and children—an extermination that did not happen, as ancient Israel certainly knew and everybody today ought to know too.

According to the first tradition-cum-theology, Israel conquered the land, with appropriate help from God. We find the extensive blocks of text for that view in Joshua 2 (the spies sent to reconnoiter the land) and Joshua 8:1—10:27 (the capture of Ai, the deal with Gibeon, and the campaign against the coalition of five kings). Traces of this view remain in the references to the kings of specific cities (see Josh 6:2; 8:2; 10:1, etc.).

According to the second tradition-cum-theology, God handled the conquest of the land, on Israel's behalf. The extensive blocks of text for this are easily located: the Jordan crossing (most of Josh 3—4), Jericho's capture (most of Josh 6), and the failed assault against Ai (most of Josh 7). The stopping of the River Jordan was something that only God could do. The collapse of the Jericho walls at a simple shout was something that only God could do. The attack on Ai, which should have been a walkover (7:3), failed because Achan disobeyed God. Success depended on God, not Israel.

According to the third tradition-cum-theology, Israel totally emptied the land of its inhabitants, men, women, and children (see especially Josh 10:28–41). The grave warnings to Israel later in the text against intermarrying with these local people and being led to worship their gods (see Josh 23, Judg 2–3, etc.) are a clear enough indication that such killing never took place. Had the locals been wiped out, the threat of intermingling would not have existed.

By now, we are used to the Bible inviting us to faith and not telling us precisely what happened. We can use the Book of Joshua to enhance our faith and deepen our theology. Which of the three views fits closest to our way of relating to our God? Do we get on with doing things and expect God to be with us in it all? (Pray as if everything depends on us.)

Do we expect God to do things in our place? (Pray as if everything depends on God.) Do we expect God to eliminate our failings and the obstacles we face? (Pray for a world free of challenge.) Which of these three styles is ours? The Book of Joshua has kept all three for us. There are values in all three. Which is ours? If we choose different styles at different times, what are our criteria?

We do not have space to talk about the total extermination of the local inhabitants. We must be free to call it what it is: appalling. In its lectionary, the Roman Church skips over Exodus 34:7. In its breviary, the Roman Church discreetly omits Psalm 137:7–9. We may give ourselves the freedom to skip over the appalling. In Joshua, what is reported—but never happened—is appalling. It never happened; even more appalling is that someone later thought it should have happened. Outrage may distract us from our own decision: do we want God to eliminate our obstacles in this imperfect world?

11. Crossing the River Jordan (Josh 3—4)

Given half a chance, some of the Joshua texts offer us the opportunity to dig deep theologically. Three questions surface : (1) do biblical texts often invite us to seek after faith rather than disclose to us the reality of knowledge? (2) do biblical texts often portray God working with us rather than instead of us? (3) what sort of texts does the Bible preserve for us?

The invitation to embrace faith is clear enough. The Bible has multiple views of creation. Israel believed that God created; obviously Israel's imagination was not shackled by a single notion of how creation had occurred. Israel believed in God's commitment, expressed after the Flood; Israel's traditions preserved different versions of that Flood. Israel believed in deliverance by God at the Reed Sea; Israel's traditions preserved conflicting ideas of what had happened there. And so on for the sojourn in the wilderness, the taking of the land, the emergence of monarchy, the efficacy of providence, and many more. The Bible usually invites to faith; it seldom imposes knowledge.

In Joshua 2, with a couple of spies sent out to reconnoiter the land, the text prepares for a campaign where God works "with us" to conquer the land. In Joshua 3—4, with the solemn processional crossing of the Jordan, the text prepares for a scenario where God works "instead of us." Both are left side by side, inviting us to think.

The signals in the text of the Jordan crossing raise the major issue of what sort of a text this is: is it reporting an event, telling a story, or rehearsing a liturgy? If rehearsing a liturgy, can some of the signals be explained as liturgical annotations and options included in the text?

We know that Israel told stories of its past, celebrated liturgies enhancing the present by recalling the past, and may have put together some of these traditions in longer sequences. These three activities are bound together in the present biblical text of the Jordan crossing. First, there is scope in plenty for storytelling. Second, we have pointers to liturgy in two explicitly liturgical acts: the placing of memorial stones in the middle of the river (Josh 4:4–7, 9); the placing of memorial stones at the place on the bank where Israel camped (4:1–3, 19–24). The catechetical affirmations associated with each memorial are different (see 4:6–7 and 4:21–24). Finally, the whole may have been part of a longer document, perhaps the Deuteronomistic History.

The text contains memories of a hurried military crossing (Josh 3:10b, 13); we know that the spies had crossed the river, presumably at the fords (2:7). The bulk of the text portrays a solemn procession, guided by the ark—and no one within a kilometer's range of it (2,000 cubits, 1,000 yards,

Josh 3:4)—with the waters stopping as the priests carrying the ark reached the river's edge, piling up at far off Adam and drying up down to the Dead Sea (3:14–17). When the people had crossed and the appropriate memorial stones had been collected, the priests with the ark emerged from their station in the middle of the Jordan bed and the waters flowed back to where they had been before.

I do not want to deny God's power to do this sort of thing. I do want to point out that the biblical text makes sense as a script and notes for the guidance of a liturgy that works through symbol. It is not repetition of what once happened but reinforcement, experienced in the present, of God's action remembered from the past. What is told in story can be celebrated in liturgy and vice versa. Liturgy and theology can contribute to wisdom, and wisdom can give insight into faith in God.

12. Capturing the City of Jericho (Josh 6)

The biblical text about Joshua's capture of Jericho is excellent for reflecting on whether God does things "with us" or "instead of us." It is also a good occasion for reflection on the sort of text that the Bible preserves for us.

The text begins with a reference to God's handing over to Joshua Jericho's "king and soldiers" (6:2). "Jericho and its king" features twice more in the book (8:2; 10:1). In the story, however, this is the last we hear of Jericho's king. Much later in the book, there is a tradition that the "citizens of Jericho" fought against Joshua (24:11). Siege, a king, and soldiers all suggest a military campaign where Israel does the fighting and God is "with them" to give them victory. There is no trace of this in the rest of chapter 6.

Instead, the text offers an odd mixture of silence and sound. Israel was to march around the city once a day for six days in total silence (see 6:10). On the seventh day, Israel was to march around the city six times in silence and on the seventh circuit, at Joshua's command, they were to shout and the walls were to collapse. Utter silence for six days and six circuits on the seventh day followed by a massive shout and collapsed walls—this would be ideal for Alfred Hitchcock, a great storyteller and a wizard with suspense. Nomadic tribes come out of the desert and face the towering stone walls of a Canaanite city. Their devastating weapon: silence. It would make for great storytelling.

On the other hand, the same text is busy making a noise. In front of the ark of the Lord, there are armed men and "seven priests with seven trumpets" blowing the trumpets continually and a rear guard following the ark, the trumpets blowing (see 6:4, 8–9, 13). With the ark, the priests and their trumpets, the soldiers and their weapons, it has the potential to be a marvelous spectacle. Imagine what Cecil B. DeMille might have made of it. Silent it certainly isn't.

For those who want an event and not a text, it is of course possible to argue that one part of the procession was blowing ritual trumpets while another part of the same procession was silent—or something of the kind. Some smoothing has occurred in the forming of a single text. Conflicting with any full harmonization, alas, is the fact that in the story two signals are given and the people's shout is reported twice (for specifying the signals: see v. 5, the trumpet blast, and v. 10, the shout; for giving the signals: see v. 16, the shout, and v. 20, the trumpet blast; for uttering the shout: see v. 20, "the people shouted" [complying with the order in v. 16] and again in v. 20, "they raised a great shout" [following the trumpet blast, also in v. 20]). Duality is dominant. The fitting of these traditions into a longer sequence is visible from the insertion of four instructions between Joshua's order to shout (v. 16) and the corresponding shout from the people (v. 20). The instructions refer to matters outside the immediate story. In all probability, the text offers us a story (silence) and a liturgy (trumpets) combined to form part of a longer narrative.

The siege, the king, and the soldiers (vv. 1–2) suggest a campaign in which Israel besieges and conquers the city, but with God's help ("See, I have handed Jericho over to you, along with its king and soldiers," v. 2). In what follows, the campaign, the king, and so forth have vanished from sight. Marching around the city might have been most effective psychological warfare, but shouts do not bring walls down—unless God does it instead of Israel. The collapse of Jericho's massive walls has little to do with Israel's action; instead of Israel's achievement with God's help, it is God's doing on Israel's behalf. The combination of both in the present text invites us to reflect theologically on how God can act in either way.

Story or liturgy, silent or noisy? What actually happened? As often, the Bible is remarkably good at keeping us in the dark. Traditions are amalgamated—or blended—rather than adjudicated. We are invited to think.

(B) ISRAEL'S LIFE IN THE LAND OF CANAAN

13. Israel's Experience of Sin and Deliverance (Judg 2—8)

Ancient Israel's theologians scrutinized three stories of its early life in the land, the stories of Ehud, of the trio Deborah, Barak, Jael (two women and one man), and of Gideon. The scrutiny is abundantly clear; how it came into existence is less clear. There are framing elements—Israel's evil, God's punishment, the people's cry, and deliverance, ending with the land's tranquility for forty years—found in full for these three stories only. That much is clear.

Preceding the Ehud story is a passage about Othniel (3:7–11) in which all the elements are brought together, but without a story to frame and with slight but significant theological differences from the framework that follows. Finally, in front of the whole text, there is an overview that spells out how the stories to follow can be understood, with differences again from the framework itself and the Othniel passage—specifying Israel's apostasy and God's anger, and speaking of judges rather than deliverers (2:11, 14–16, 18–19).

From a developmental point of view, the process of reflective growth may well have begun with the framing elements drawing the stories together, been refined in the Othniel passage, and reached culmination in the overview as theological ideas were developed. From a final-form point of view, the sequence of the biblical text may be followed, with the overview explaining the rest and therefore to be taken for granted in what follows, echoed in part by what is said in the Othniel passage, and brought to mind regularly in the subsequent framing. What matters for us, as so often, is not certainty about the process by which the text came into being, but awareness of the insight, intelligence, and intensity that went into the production of such texts. What is then important for us is to profit from the product, the biblical text we have, remaining aware that reflective processes gave us the text we have.

The experiences rehearsed in these three stories were carefully worked over in ancient Israel, with the basic insights from the experiences told in the stories apparently refined at least twice. What is particularly galling for us is that, after all that, we are left unsure at the most basic level as to what was learned as primary from the experience. Was it that God could be relied on to deliver Israel from its punishment? Was it that Israel could be relied on to abandon its God and be punished by that God? Where are we today in all this?

Certainly, God is portrayed punishing Israel for its evil (3:12–14; 4:2; 6:1). Certainly, God is portrayed—at much greater length—delivering Israel from its punishment. In the three stories, Israel suffered lengthy foreign oppression and was freed from it by the military action of these leader figures. Equally certain, in the portrayal, Israel's freedom lasted a generation and then Israel lapsed into repeated evil. While modern commentators have emphasized God's deliverance of Israel, they have been less eager to point out that God is portrayed inflicting the oppression on Israel as punishment for its evil. Nor are these commentators eager to point out that the appropriate structures did not exist in Israel to prevent these repeated lapses.

We are left to wonder what is important here: that God delivered repentant Israel from the oppression with which God had punished it or, on the other hand, that delivered Israel regularly relapsed into evildoing which evoked punishment? As we have learned to expect, the biblical text does not make our choices for us; perhaps no choice is to be made, with both aspects important.

It is not surprising that the overview and 3:7–11 should identify Israel's evil as apostasy. The fundamental infidelity of apostasy bedeviled Israel throughout its scriptures; it is a temptation alive among us today. It is not surprising—though it may not be good theology—that the text attributes to God both the power to cause Israel's oppression and then to enable Israel to subdue its oppressors. It is somewhat surprising that the God to whom this power is attributed is not given the power to prevent Israel from relapsing into evil.

For Israel, did the theology extracted from these stories speak primarily of God's power to punish? Or of God's readiness to deliver? Or did the theology extracted from these stories speak of Israel's incapacity to resist the allure of evil? For us today, it is important to reflect on our experiences and situations. How do we cope with recurring evil? How do we cope with forgiveness? How do we account for tyranny and oppression, whether in a single household or a global world?

14. Ehud (Judg 3)

In the first part of the Book of Judges we find the three stories of bravery, held together by the interpretative framing just discussed. The three stories may be read as examples of God's repeated deliverance or of repeated human infidelity—or both. Israel extracted theology from its experience. The stories tell the experience; as we have seen, the framing extracts the theology. Having looked at the process and the theology, it is time to look at the stories themselves as repositories of experience from which theology can emerge.

The first story is about Ehud (Judg 3:15–29; its framing is in 3:12–15a and 30). The story tells of considerable bravery. Ehud assassinated a Moabite despot who had been oppressing Israel for eighteen years. We live at a time that is sickened by random violence. Whether we go back to the anarchists around the beginning of World War I or whether we focus on the surfeit of killing in recent years, the political assassin is viewed with contempt, except by fellow fanatics. Even the carefully targeted killing of a foreign oppressor is not an action that elicits our sympathies. Different times had different views. Especially when petty despots abounded, assassination was a means of last resort and heroes resorted to it.

Ehud was the leader of the delegation that delivered Israel's tribute to Eglon, king of Moab—presumably at Jericho, "the city of palms" (v. 13). This was tax paid to a foreign tyrant; we are entitled to assume that it was felt as oppressive extortion. The Bible thinks so: "the Israelites served King Eglon of Moab eighteen years" (v. 14).

After the tribute had been handed over, the Israelite delegation left the king. At some distance from the city (v. 19), Ehud turned back and reappeared in the royal presence. It is typical of Israelite storytelling that the text does not say why; we are left to think for ourselves. Did Ehud believe that by coming back he had a better chance of being alone with the king? Had Ehud lost his nerve at the last minute and only later regained his courage? Was he protecting the fellow members of the delegation and giving them a chance to get away? Was the sword he had strapped to his right thigh, being left-handed, standard practice, and did he only see the opening for assassination at the last minute? We do not know. The text leaves it to us—or the storyteller in ancient Israel—to fill it out as we see best, if we want to.

Two observations on the story. First, Ehud's action was one of great bravery. He might easily have been searched and disarmed by cautious guards. The king might not have dismissed his attendants. Ehud risked his life and was lucky to get away with it. Second, killing the Moabite king left the Moabites leaderless and lifted Israelite morale. It enabled Ehud to raise troops in Israel's hill country, cut off the Moabite invaders, and so free Israel from eighteen years' oppression. Where does the biblical text see God's action in all this? Does it have to be miraculous to be marvelous?

Two comments on the framing material. First, God "strengthened King Eglon of Moab against Israel, because they had done what was evil in the sight of the Lord" (v. 12). Reflection: what sort of theology is this and how sound do we find it? Second, God raised up Ehud as a deliverer for Israel (v. 15). Reflection: God's action does not rate a mention in the story. Intriguing; the framers claim insight the storyteller did not have.

15. Deborah–Barak–Jael (Judg 4—5)

In the last passage, we looked at the story of Ehud, assassin and deliverer of Israel. In this one, we look at three figures associated with one victory: Deborah, Barak, and Jael. There are similarities; there are differences.

According to the framing material, Israel went back to doing evil when Ehud died and, as a consequence, God "sold them into the hand" of the Canaanites. The oppression was cruel and it lasted for twenty years (4:1–3). The pattern is similar; it comes from the framing material. The differences begin in the story. In contrast to Ehud, Deborah had an official role; she was a prophetess and judged Israel (4:4). We have no information about her role as judge, just as we have no knowledge of what the prophet Samuel's role as judge involved (1 Sam 7:15–17), to say nothing of the role of his sons as judges in Beer-sheba (1 Sam 8:1–3). Barak too had a job. It is clear from the story that he was a senior commander of the Israelite forces; he could summon tribes and warriors to gather under his command (4:10). Jael had no job, no official position; she was not even an Israelite, but a Kenite. Yet it is Jael who, in the text, performs the climactic act of great bravery: she assassinates Sisera, the Canaanite general.

The differences continue. Deborah, the woman, tells Barak, the military chief, what God commands him to do. Perhaps that is her role as prophetess. Most surprisingly, Barak refuses to obey unless Deborah will go with him; he makes her participation a condition of his obedience to God. I am not aware of any military figure taking a similar stance elsewhere in the Bible. In the text, Deborah makes quite sure Barak knows just how invidious his position is going to be. He will win victory, but he will not win glory; the enemy general will be killed by a woman (4:9).

The next difference in this story is that the military victory is won with explicit help from God. Nothing was said to this effect in the Ehud story. Here, in Deborah's message, Barak is promised victory by God (4:7). On the day of battle, Deborah assures Barak that God will give him victory

(4:14). In the battle, God does just that, throwing the Canaanite army into a panic (4:15).

Much closer to the Ehud story is the account of how Jael killed the fugitive Sisera. She drove a tent peg through his head as he slept. We have only to release our imaginations from the certainties of canonical text to realize how immensely brave this was. Had a trace of nervous sweat caused her hand to slip on the tent peg or the mallet, had anything awakened the sleeping soldier, he would have killed her instantly—probably strangled her with one hand. Instead, he died, and God is not mentioned.

Israel's storyteller-theologians are forcing us to think. God gave Barak victory over the Canaanite army. Unprompted and unaided, Jael disposed of the Canaanite general with a tent peg. Where does that leave us theologically?

At the end of the story, the land was "quiet" or "undisturbed" for forty years, usually understood as a generation (5:31). After Ehud, the figure is eighty years (3:30), generally reckoned to include forty years associated with Shamgar. The theological problem: the acts of deliverance are wonderful, but what is happening that Israel falls back into evil again after a generation? Something is amiss here—or regrettably and typically human.

16. Gideon (Judg 6–8)

After Moabites and Canaanites, it is the turn of the Midianites to oppress Israel for seven years (6:1). The deliverer was to be Gideon. Like Ehud, Gideon had no particular office in Israel. The text has him highly distrustful of himself: "My clan is the weakest in Manasseh, and I am the least in my family" (6:15). In sharp contrast to Ehud, Gideon has regular communications with angels and with God. The text also has Gideon highly distrustful of God; he tests God twice to be sure that he, Gideon, is to deliver Israel (6:36–40; wet fleece and dry ground, dry fleece and wet ground). His doubts are still to the fore on the night of his attack on the oppressing Midianites. His fears are overcome when, in the enemy camp, he hears a soldier interpreting another's dream to foretell Gideon's victory (7:9–14).

The Gideon story is probably best known for the episode in which his own troops were drastically reduced in number. The fearful were sent home. The rest were sorted out by the way they drank from the water of the spring. The cautious, who knelt to drink from cupped hands, were sent home; the three hundred who lapped up the water, as dogs do, were kept. At first sight, and as the story tells it, this action demanded Gideon's total trust in God. "The Lord said to Gideon, 'The troops with you are too many for me to give the Midianites into their hand. Israel would only take the credit away from me, saying, "My own hand has delivered me"'" (7:2).

Closer inspection of the story allows for a military understanding. Gideon's troops executed a night attack on the enemy camp, using trumpets and flares to spread panic and confusion and put the enemy to rout (7:20–21). In today's armies, with night-vision goggles, hand-held radios, and all the high-tech paraphernalia of communications, a night attack of this kind would be a relatively standard commando-type operation, even if needing careful preparation. For the ancients, such a night attack would have been extremely risky. It would have only needed one frightened or clumsy soldier to stumble and the alarm would have been raised and the enemy camp alerted. Gideon divided his troops into three companies of a hundred each. If one jumped the gun before the others were in position, the element of surprise would have been lost. It was a high-risk strategy, demanding extreme courage, and best carried out by a minimum number of very tough troops. Was the theological reason a cover? The text does not suggest it, but a storyteller might.

Gideon's tactics worked. The battle was a rout. Like Ehud, Gideon called in others to chase out the oppressors. In the Ehud story, however, God was not mentioned; in the Gideon traditions, by contrast, God is intimately involved. Different theologies?

Other traditions have been associated with those of Gideon's victory over the Midianite camp. We can prescind from them here, but two fragments are worth mentioning. Early in the piece, Gideon was celebrated as the hero who tore down Ophrah's altar of Baal, source of apostasy in Israel (6:25–32). Almost at the end of the Gideon traditions, there is a strange tradition that, in the same town of Ophrah, Gideon set up a cult object that involved all Israel in apostasy (8:24–27). Strange, contrary to expectation, and pointing perhaps to the flaws found in so many leaders—the final part of Lord Acton's dictum: great men are seldom good men.

REFLECTIVE MOMENTS
FOR PART THREE

It would seem that what is narrated in the first part of the Book of Joshua does not correlate with anything we can say about Israel's occupation of the land of Canaan. Am I relieved or worried?

≈

Where am I in all this? How do I understand God in all this? Does God do things for me? Does God help me do things for myself? Did I ever envisage God setting Canaan to rights once and for all? Am I grieved that God has not set my world to rights? Do I expect God to do so? Am I content for God simply to be with me in it all?

When we look at the portrayal of Israel's life in the land of Canaan in the first part of the Book of Judges, we have the ups and downs of tribal survival correlated with God's punishment and God's deliverance. Does that correspond with my own experience? Is it a theology that I find acceptable? Do I find myself applying it to my life? How do I understand the place of God in the ups and downs of my own experience?

Reflective Activity

Look at or imagine a painting that depicts some of the scenes here. Notice what is happening in you as you observe.

PART FOUR:
Private Image and Public Power

DAVID: ISRAEL'S GREAT KING

Introduction

The two Books of Samuel are filled with the figure of David. Later Israel held David in high regard. Throughout 1 Samuel, although described as "a man after his [God's] own heart," David is depicted struggling, destined for the crown but not yet in possession of it.

The latter part of 2 Samuel deals with David as king and the potential for both great achievement and great folly, even evil, involved in unfettered power. The stories in 2 Samuel 11—20 are widely regarded as some of the Bible's best. A quality that runs through all of them is the insight they offer into human motivation, not so much by pointing to issues or asking questions about them, but by leaving critical readers to uncover their own questions and wonder about them. As such, the stories are brilliant.

17. David and the Philistine (1 Sam 17)

Few Bible stories have gripped the popular imagination as has the story of David and Goliath—and, alas, the popular imagination all too often gets it regrettably wrong. In popular parlance, a "David and Goliath" situation has the small and powerless facing and overcoming the big and powerful—against all odds. Great stuff, but not the stuff of the Bible story.

The story of David and the Philistine champion—"Goliath" is used twice, "the Philistine" some thirty times—is about trust in God, certainly, but about that sort of trust in God that enables us to do what we have the capacities and abilities to do.

We should not underestimate David. He may have been the youngest son and a good-looking redhead; so is many a hefty hunk. Saul says to him, "you are just a boy" (17:33). It sounds conclusive, but it is a miserable example of misleading translation. In the context, it means "inexperienced"—the recent recruit compared with the grizzled veteran. The same Hebrew word (*na'ar* = boy/youth) has a wide range of meaning, from an infant in arms (e.g., 1 Sam 1:22) to a soldier in military service (e.g., 2 Sam 18:15) to a minister of the king (e.g., 1 Kgs 11:28). It is used of dependents, irrespective of age, including those still in the family household, in the army, or in the service of the king. In the immediate context, this same Hebrew word is used for *all* Jesse's sons in 16:11 ("Are they all here?"). In a family of sons, we might perhaps ask, "Are all the boys here?"—even when they range in age from twenty to forty—and we are well aware that they stopped being boys long ago. The three eldest of Jesse's sons were serving in Saul's army (17:13). Nothing so far to suggest that David was barred by age or size.

David's own description of himself is worth scrutiny. He says that, when he was a shepherd, if a lion or bear took a lamb from the flock, he would go after it, strike it, and rescue the lamb from its mouth, and if it turned on him he would grab it by the jaw, strike it, and kill it (17:34–35). He'd catch it, so he was fast. He'd strike it and get the lamb back, so he had courage. If attacked, he'd grab it by the jaw and kill it, so he was not only tough and ruthless but had very good reflexes. This is no "small, apparently defenseless" shepherd boy. We often think of shepherds as "cuddlers" of lambs; they also had the role of "killers" of predators when the flock needed protection.

We should not underestimate David's weapon. The sling was a standard military weapon (see 2 Kgs 3:25 and 2 Chron 26:14); the sling was a very accurate weapon (see Judg 20:16). This is no schoolboy's slingshot or catapult; it played the same fearful role in the ancient world as the longbow on behalf of the English against the French cavalry at the battles of Crecy and Agincourt or the Molotov cocktail against the German tank in World War II. In hand-to-hand combat, the giant Philistine was probably unbeatable; at a distance, the sling was the ideal weapon to take him out—especially if his armor-bearer was still holding his shield for him (17:41).

All David had to do was to get within range and not miss. He knew he could do it, as long as he didn't lose his nerve and mess up. He could stumble and fall in the approach run; he could miss with his first shot and probably not get a second—he'd be dead. So he put his trust in God all right and he did what he knew he could do. The Philistine ended up dead instead.

Far better than having God help the hopeless, the story speaks to God helping the able, whether the hopeful or the hesitant, those who need encouragement and support, enabling them to do what they are able to do—with a little encouragement, support, and readiness to risk.

Incidentally, there are two stories in 1 Samuel 17 about this single combat between David and the Philistine. Both are in the Hebrew text; only one is in the Greek. In the second one (above all, 17:12–30; 17:55—18:5; 18:17–19,

29b–30), David is ambitious; trust in God takes a back seat. "What shall be done for the man who kills this Philistine?" (17:26). Great wealth, a king's daughter in marriage, and tax-free status for the family.

Ambition and faith. No harm in combining them both.

18. David and Bathsheba (2 Sam 11—12)

The next four stories we will explore come from 2 Samuel 11—20; they are quite unusual within the biblical repertoire. All four offer the possibility of exploring human motivation, what makes human beings tick, and what makes them go wrong. The stories leave multiple avenues open to the imagination; they close none. To explain why these stories have this characteristic would take up space we do not have; it is enough to say that they do.

The story of David and Bathsheba is well known and frequently referred to as David's adultery. That is most unfair to the woman and to the biblical text. Adultery today implies consent: "voluntary sexual intercourse"; today, without consent, it is rape. The biblical text gives no indication whatsoever of anything approaching invitation from David or consent from Bathsheba. David takes her; we know no more. She was washing; from the palace roof, he was looking; she was very beautiful. We know no more. There is no suggestion whatsoever of immodesty on her part. David should have known better; she was the wife of one of his soldiers.

We can imagine possibilities for her wants and his; the text says nothing. Bathsheba's announcement of her pregnancy calls for reflection and receives none in the text. "She sent and told David, 'I am pregnant.'" (11:5). At opposite poles are two possibilities: "I am pregnant, my darling" or "I am pregnant, you bastard." In either case, why tell him? The text sheds no light. The possibilities are not explored, although she needs protection and so does he. If there is love, they may have discussed the possibilities. If there is hatred, she may have considered the risk worth running. The text is silent. Two options for her: to lie low and keep it out of the public eye; alternatively, to tell him (which she does). Two for him: to keep it out of the public eye (for example, by having her killed, sent into the country, etc.); alternatively, to marry her (which he does, after having her husband killed). Why did she tell him?

The next move calls for just as much reflection and again the text provides none. Immediately, David sends to Joab for Uriah, her husband (11:6). The options open to David were many; they are not discussed in the text—he sent for Uriah. What did David hope for from Uriah's coming to Jerusalem? Why did Uriah refuse royal orders and sleep so publicly at the palace? Of the many involved, who knew and how much did they know? What did Uriah know and what did he want? Was Uriah too trusting, too angry, or too greedy and ambitious? Did he not think David capable of strategic killing? We do not know and the text does not tell us. Instead, all we know is that David had Uriah killed at the battlefront, courtesy of Joab.

With Uriah dead, and out of the way, David moves to marriage with Bathsheba. The marriage does not decide between earlier options; issues of love, public image, and kingly status are too intermingled to allow for clarity. With the marriage, one might expect the story to move to closure. A half-verse indicates that closure is not in reach: "the thing that David had done displeased the Lord" (11:27b). There is more to come and come it will. Kings have power and power has limits, whether in the eyes of God or the unfolding of history. God sends Nathan; history unfolds.

What on earth is this story doing in sacred scripture? We can learn from it of the capacity in ancient times to spin a complex story. We can learn that a king guilty of sexual crime and murder can be construed as God's model king. David was sinful but faithful. There can be hope for us.

19. David and Amnon (2 Sam 13)

Recently a friend read over a manuscript for me. I had written of Judges 19—21 that they were among "the strangest and most unpleasant" chapters in all of biblical literature. She wrote in the margin: too soft—totally abhorrent. I settled for "the most abominable." This story of Amnon and Tamar is both abhorrent and abominable. Because it is in our Bible makes it no less abhorrent and abominable. It is a good example of God's needing to write straight with some very crooked lines.

Tamar, David's daughter, was a beautiful woman (13:1). Amnon, David's eldest son, fell in love with her and "made himself ill" because of her, thinking she was totally out of his reach—a virgin princess at the royal court. Jonadab, a friend of Amnon's and a nephew of David's, is described as "a very wise man" (Hebrew; not to be transformed to "a very crafty man"). Wisdom can be used for bad ends as well as good. Jonadab is a thoroughly bad egg. He asks a few questions; he has noticed Amnon looking "haggard morning after morning" (13:4). Amnon tells of his passion for the inaccessible Tamar. Jonadab suggests a scheme to get her within Amnon's reach: ask King David to have her come over and bake some cakes for poor Amnon in his sickness.

At this point, we start asking some questions. The scheme is absurd; David will not have a bar of it. So why does Jonadab bring it up? A possible scenario is unspeakable—but unfortunately not unthinkable. At least, we'd think it of many a modern despot (Idi Amin, Pol Pot, Saddam Hussein, Stalin, etc.). Could David have been in the same league? Alas, it is possible. He did order Uriah's murder and married his widow. The unspeakable scenario: Jonadab is acting on a suggestion from David. After all, the king needs as his heir the smartest of his two eldest sons. Creating bad blood between them might be one way of finding out which has what it takes to be king. Absalom, the second son, happens to be Tamar's full brother, not a half-brother like Amnon. Planned or not, it works out that way. In two years, Absalom has his revenge and murders Amnon.

Diabolical or not, David was slack. When Amnon's request for Tamar's culinary services was made, all David needed to do was send a burly soldier with her, under orders not to let her out of his sight for a moment. David did not. Instead, he sent Tamar to her fate.

According to the story, Amnon ordered everybody out of the room after Tamar had arrived. What a pity that burly soldier was not there, with his orders from the king. Instead, everybody left. There was no social solidarity whatsoever to support Tamar. The poor woman was on her own.

The text treats her with the greatest respect. She is the only figure with any nobility in the entire story. That does not change her fate—the story is abhorrent and abominable. Amnon demands sex. She names what he wants as "vile." She spells out its implications for her and for him. She offers him a possible way out: ask the king, "for he will not withhold me from you" (vv. 12–13). "But he would not listen to her; and being stronger than she, he forced her and lay with her" (v. 14). He orders her out into the street. Absalom meets her and counsels silence. David is reported to have known; he does nothing. Two years later, Absalom has Amnon killed.

It is an appalling story, told without whitewashing any of the sordid details. I can't make anything encouraging out of it—except that the Bible portrays evil as evil and doesn't try to turn a blind eye to it.

20. David and Absalom (2 Sam 15—19)

The last story was abominable. While this one may delight us with detail, I am afraid that the central question is just as unpleasant. Absalom, David's heir, runs a rebellion against his father and is killed in battle. The question: was David involved in the killing of his son? The issue: whether David was coldly ruthless or besottedly naive. A credible soft option does not seem to exist.

Overtly, the text is quite explicit on the subject: David did not want his son Absalom killed. Very publicly, as the troops were going out to battle, he is reported giving specific orders to the three commanders, "Deal gently for my sake with the young man Absalom" (18:5). All the army heard. As overtly, according to the narrative, Absalom was happy to have his father dead (17:1–4) and David knew it: "my own son seeks my life" (16:11). Fathers put up with these aberrations from their sons; ruling despots are not so tolerant of their rivals. There was a middle road: to have kept Absalom out of the kingdom after the killing of Amnon. But David had abandoned that course when, under Joab's urging, he brought Absalom back from exile—but avoided a reconciliation for too long.

The text of 2 Samuel 15—19 is extraordinary. It portrays one of the decisive moments of Israel's national existence: will King David fall victim to his son? What will become of God's vision if he does? The biblical narrative is detailed either side of the encounter; it follows David down to the Jordan and it follows him back. What happens across the Jordan is of little importance in the unfolding narrative. The battle between the king's men and Absalom's rebels is given three verses (18:6–8). The actual killing of Absalom is given seven (18:9–15). The carrying of the message of Absalom's death to David and his reaction to it are given twenty-three verses (18:19—19:9 [NRSV, 19:8]). The statistics here do not mislead; the narrative does not linger on the battle or the killing. Why is the text so detailed where we do not expect it to be?

For many, David's lament is immensely powerful, emotionally: "O my son Absalom, my son, my son Absalom!" (Heb. 19:1; NRSV, 18:33; also 19:5; NRSV, 19:4). What an appalling possibility that the lament may be utterly cynical—a political exercise in spin. Or do fathers who have ordered the deaths of their sons grieve all the same? Or did Joab order the killing on his own initiative because he judged it needed to be done?

The detail provided is intensely focused; the gaps in the information given us are vast. We know Absalom spent four years fomenting and organizing the rebellion; we know almost nothing about what he did and how he did it. The news of the revolt was brought to David, and he decided instantly to abandon the allegedly impregnable city of Jerusalem—and we are not told why. David sent the ark back into Jerusalem with total trust in God; in the same breath, through the priests of the ark he planned a communications network to keep him informed. David prayed to the Lord to defeat the counsel of Ahithophel and promptly instructed Hushai to be his double agent against Ahithophel. For David, prayer and politics went hand in hand. David's faith: leave nothing to God except trust.

The biggest gap of all is why the Lord's anointed came so close to being overthrown. David and his mercenaries fled across the Jordan. Absalom had the unwitting support of two hundred notables from Jerusalem (15:11); he had well-informed supporters "throughout all the tribes of Israel" (15:10). We do not know why David fled or why Absalom had such support. We may suspect neglect of justice (15:1–6); we know no details. With Absalom dead and the revolt crushed, debate is reported raging in Israel and Judah as to whether to bring David back as king.

In all of this, politics was at work; in all of this, the narrative claims God was at work ("the Lord had ordained," 17:14b). Human action and divine action are inextricably interwoven. This David was a great king; he is God's chosen, Israel's model. He was a skilled politician, an inspirer of men—and a flawed human being. The Bible holds together both aspects. God may well write straight, but certainly with crooked lines.

21. David and Joab (2 Sam 20)

The fragility of David's kingdom is evident in this episode. It may be a symbol of the fragility of God's enterprise on this earth. The episode is a lesson in the politics of power.

No sooner had Absalom's revolt been defeated, with David on the verge of resuming his role as king in Jerusalem, than the text portrays a single individual's call to rebellion being heeded by the bulk of the people—"the people of Israel withdrew from David...the people of Judah followed their king" (20:2).

What lay behind the rivalry of Israel and Judah, reported at the end of chapter 19, escapes us. Whatever was at stake, Judah won, but David lost the loyalty of the other tribes, of northern Israel. Joab had led the civil war against Abner and Ishbaal for David; he had sabotaged a possible peace, killing his rival, Abner. He had organized Uriah's killing for David. He had organized Absalom's return from exile. He had killed Absalom. Whether Joab knew too much, had too much power, or had earned David's displeasure, we do not know; we do know that he had been replaced as army commander by Amasa, whose power base was Judah. With the unity, and perhaps the very existence, of his kingdom threatened, David gave Amasa a three-day mission: call out the troops from Judah to be at David's service (20:4).

According to the text, Amasa took more than the three days allotted for his mission. Tardiness or treason? We are not told. David now gave the top military job to Abishai, Joab's brother—not to Joab. Abishai led the mercenaries north, after Sheba's rebels; the indispensable Joab went along. Abishai had not gone very far—to Gibeon, just north of Jerusalem—when Amasa came up with the expedition. Nothing is said of the troops Amasa was supposed to have raised. Joab did to Amasa what he had done to Abner: drew him close and thrust a sword into his belly.

With Amasa dead, the march resumed. The text is abrupt, but Joab has resumed command. Amasa's body was spooking the troops, so one of Joab's men dragged it away from the road and threw a cloak over it. The march went on.

Sheba, the leader of the rebels, had holed up in the walled town of Abel, near Israel's northern border. Joab proceeded to siege operations. A "wise woman" spared the town the savagery of siege by negotiating first with Joab, then with the townspeople. The outcome: Sheba's head was thrown over the wall, and Joab's troops dispersed and went home. "Joab returned to Jerusalem to the king" (20:22).

The story of Sheba's revolt can stand for most of the Davidic stories. It is a brutal story from start to finish. Joab loses his job; Amasa loses his life. Amasa's body is taken off the road; Sheba's head is tossed over the town wall. Joab returns to Jerusalem to the king. David had fired him; Joab had reinstated himself. Whose was the real power?

David has been described from the outset as a man after God's own heart (1 Sam 13:14) and has been promised lasting power in Israel (2 Sam 7:16). He will keep that power and one of his line will exercise it in Judah to the very end. Israel's theologians knew its seamy side and were not squeamish about associating God with David. The Davidic texts give incarnation an undreamed of intensity. Faith sets

God on transcendent heights; faith also claims God's presence in the innermost activity of human minds and hearts.

REFLECTIVE MOMENTS FOR PART FOUR

David and the Philistine (1 Sam 17)

The present text of the story allows for both ambitious realism ("What shall be done for the man who kills this Philistine?") and faith ("the Lord will deliver you into my hand"). Christian tradition has long opted to see the Lord take the side of the powerless against the powerful and enable the unprepared David to overcome the mighty Goliath. Does my preference lie with David's faith or David's sling? Is there a place for both?

David and Bathsheba (2 Sam 11—12)

One biblical scholar wrote: "The narrator performs the function of a camera, slowing [sic] panning over the female body. The first frame reveals the length of her entire naked body at her bath." How refreshing to discover that the biblical narrator doesn't engage in anything of the kind. How appalling to realize how almost unanimously interpreters have betrayed the biblical text and blamed Bathsheba. Where does that leave me? Whom do I blame? What responsibilities does this raise for me in how I report situations? What cautions does it raise about how the media reports situations?

David and Amnon (2 Sam 13)

Whatever David's motivation may have been, it was foolishly improper to have sent Tamar to his son without a bodyguard. How do I feel about the foolishness of a model king? If there has been such foolishness in my own living, what might have motivated it?

~

David and Absalom (2 Sam 15—19)

Absalom wanted David dead so that he might be king in his father's place. Given this, how do I see the portrayal of David, wanting his murderous son spared: as heroic, as foolish and soft, or as unpleasantly smart and politically ruthless?

~

David and Joab (2 Sam 20)

David demoted Joab from the army command. Joab won the campaign and returned in charge of the army. Whose plans were operative here? Do I think in terms of "the plans of God"? What part do I attribute to power politics and what to God?

~

All of these issues can show the political moves of a man of faith and realism. Can my faith accommodate such realism? Israel's tradition managed to hold both.

Reflective Activity

Read a poem that expresses faith and realism. Notice what happens in you as you ponder.

PART FIVE:
Faith, Fidelity, and Justice

ISRAEL AND THE PROPHETS

Introduction

Israel's prophecy, at least its preexilic prophecy, is a rare phenomenon, unheard of elsewhere. It lasted a couple of hundred years, from around 750 to around 550 BCE. It had forerunners and follow-up; nevertheless it had an identity all its own.

(A) Prophetic Stories: Confronting the King. Prophecy's forerunners in ancient Israel are to be found principally in the Books of Samuel–Kings. Jewish tradition speaks of "former" and "latter" prophets, with Joshua–Kings termed "former prophets"; Christian tradition has referred to these as the "historical books." Neither way of speaking is fully satisfactory. Not "former prophets": prophets such as Samuel and Nathan, Elijah and Elisha, play a major part in Samuel–Kings, but there are no equivalents in Joshua and Judges. Not "historical books": among other things, Joshua–Kings deal with contemporary political and theological issues associated with their times; they are not concerned to provide the history of their times.

In any society, unbridled power needs bridling—preferably by powerful movements, institutions, or figures giving voice to the conscience of the people. Readers will know their own examples from recent times. In ancient Israel, three moments are recorded within Samuel–Kings, where prophets confronted kings; prophets: Samuel, Nathan, and Elijah on one side and kings: Saul, David, and Ahab on the other. As single confrontations between individuals, these episodes could be preserved in story form. At a later time, beginning with Hosea and Amos, prophets confronted their nations, Israel (the northern kingdom) and Judah (the southern kingdom); these activities could not be confined to single stories but generated the prophetic books.

(B) Prophetic Truth: Confronting the Issue. In any age, the question confronts society: who is speaking our conscience? Who is right about our future? Who names the reality of our present? Who are our prophets? Where do we look for the truth we need?

The answers to these questions have never been simple and have seldom been clear. In this, Israel was no different from any other society. Obedience, orthodoxy, fulfillment, common sense, insight, presence in the councils of God all played their role. Certainty was not to replace faith, but the stories in which Israel confronted the issue are fascinating.

The three stories we look at here treat the issue in quite different ways. All three generated marvelous one-liners. At Bethel: "you have disobeyed God, you will not make it to your family grave." From Micaiah: "if you return in peace, the Lord has not spoken by me." From Jeremiah: "before the end of the year, you will be dead"—and he was. Great rhetoric and good one-liners do not necessarily resolve problems; Israel had the grace to know it had the problems.

(C) Prophetic Books: Confronting the People. Israel's so-called writing prophets did not sit down and write books; they went out in the streets and confronted people. Jeremiah 36 may not be historical, but it provides a fair picture of how many understood prophetic books to have been put together.

Israel appears to have had a sense of what the prophetic experience had to communicate. Three elements predominated: oracles directed against God's own people (within these: accusations of wrong linked to announcements of consequences); oracles against Israel's enemies; oracles of hope for a future time. Two factors were particularly pilloried by the prophets: religious infidelity and social injustice. Fidelity to their God was essential to national survival. Justice went hand in hand with being God's people. Infidelity and injustice were named by the prophets in various ways as reasons for God to move against Israel, and were factors inexorably eroding Israel from within.

(A) PROPHETIC STORIES: CONFRONTING THE KING

22. Samuel and King Saul (1 Sam 15)

This is a cautionary tale rather than a historical report; it imposes a limit on royal power, insists on the king's duty of obedience to God, and warns of the consequences of neglecting that duty. The prophet Samuel speaks for God; the king is Saul. At its highpoint are three terse words in Hebrew (two trisyllables and one thumping monosyllable): *shemoa mizevach tov,* colloquially: obedience better'n sacrifice (15:22).

The Amalekites were a group to the south of Israel, listed as descended from Esau (Gen 36:12, 16). They confronted Israel in a highly symbolic battle on Israel's way to Mount Sinai, a battle the Amalekites lost, but that did not end hostilities (Exod 17:8–16). They came under Balaam's curse (Num 24:20). In the early chapters of Judges, they teamed with various enemies to make life miserable for Israel (cf. Judg 3:13; 6:3, 33; 7:12; 10:12). Deuteronomy came down on them hard: "you shall blot out the remembrance of Amalek from under heaven; do not forget" (Deut 25:19).

Against this background, Samuel gives Saul his mission: wipe out the Amalekites; "utterly destroy all that they have" (15:3). "Utterly destroy" translates the Hebrew verb for "put to the ban"; the ban would appear to have been ultimately a religious concept. When a ban was declared, no booty was to be taken. The ban meant that the war party was to make no profit from plunder or captives; it was a symbol that all was done for God alone. Saul is pictured leading a major expedition against the Amalekites, taking their king captive and utterly destroying them all. Well, almost all. Not only did Saul and the people spare King Agag; they also kept the best of the livestock and all that was valuable. The ban was not observed.

Aware of this, Samuel goes looking for Saul. When they meet, Saul gets off to a bad start; his greeting: "May you be blessed by the Lord; I have carried out the command of the Lord." Says Samuel: What are the sounds of animals I hear? Says Saul, passing the buck: Ah yes, "the people spared the best of livestock to sacrifice to the Lord *your* God" (15:15). The attempt by "the man" in the Garden to pass the buck to God ("the woman whom *you* gave to be with me" [Gen 3:12]) echoes here.

Samuel is not bought off by a bit of manipulative language. He puts Saul firmly on the spot: you have a high position and the responsibility that goes with it. You were given a job with specific conditions. Why did you disobey and succumb to greed? (see 15:17–19). Saul makes one last try: I have obeyed. I've brought Agag, their king, here. I've utterly destroyed the Amalekites, taking no captives, and the people have brought the best of the animals, the best of what should have been devoted to God, to sacrifice to *your* God here in Gilgal (see 15:20–21).

It is good storytelling and a good try by Saul. Samuel is not fooled. Out come those terrible words: *"shemoa mizevach tov,"* "to obey is better than sacrifice"; you have rejected the word of the Lord, the Lord has rejected you from being king (15:22).

Saul says, "I have sinned," and Samuel won't have any of it (1 Sam 15:24–26). Later, David will say, "I have sinned," and Nathan says, "The Lord has put away your sin" (2 Sam 12:13). Subtle casuistry can be brought into play, the word of the Lord versus the moral law, and that sort of thing. The reality is that we do not know why forgiveness was available to David and not to Saul. History, however, required that Saul be rejected and that David continue as king.

In this story, we are in the realm of theology, not history. We know that a little later David's camp at Ziklag will be the victim of an Amalekite raid and in the subsequent engagement only four hundred of the Amalekite camel corps will escape David's revenge (1 Sam 30). So much for Saul's having destroyed them all. The last we hear of them at this point is in the summary of David's victories (2 Sam 8:12).

Theology and human values require that the powers of any central authority be limited, be subject to an overriding power, here named God. That overriding power is not ceded to any office. It is remarkable that, in its culture, Israel could make this claim to impose a limit on its kings.

23. Nathan and King David (2 Sam 12)

This story is another classic case of a prophet's confrontation with the reigning monarch. Saul was sacked; David retains his crown, but the consequences of his actions are spelled out. The inevitable question: is Nathan's speech to David a prediction of what is to come or a reflection on what has already happened? Within the text as we have it, there is no doubt: it is prediction. Within the same present text, there are no indicators to contradict this, beyond the somewhat muddled intertwining of its two strands. Unfortunately, the absence of clear indicators is not an infallible guide. The reality also has to be taken into account that almost all texts are composed later than the happenings with which they are involved. The truth, however, is simple; prediction or reflection: we do not know. What is remarkable and not to be overlooked: the culture allowed for the text.

The context is well known (see 2 Sam 11:2–27). King David had intercourse with Bathsheba, the wife of one of his soldiers, a woman whose name he did not know as of late afternoon on the day he slept with her. Informed that she had become pregnant, he tried to have Uriah, her husband, cover for him in her bed. When this failed, he had the man killed and in due course married the woman. The child was a son.

In the narrative, as we have it, the text of the confrontation has elements of two distinct strands in relation to what David had done. David, as king, saw to it that Uriah was killed; one strand is concerned with the consequences. David, as king, gave free rein to his sexual urges and violated another's marriage; the second strand is concerned with the consequences.

According to the biblical text, the Lord sent Nathan the prophet to confront David the king. Nathan began with a parable featuring a rich man with extensive flocks and a poor man with one little ewe lamb; rather than slaughtering an animal from his own herds, the rich man requisitioned the poor man's one lamb to feed a guest. Says David indignantly: "the man who has done this deserves to die." Says Nathan: "you are the man" (2 Sam 12:6–7).

The text then has Nathan unfold the consequences. According to him, David had been given Saul's wives and God would have added anything else he wanted—all of which the Davidic texts do not mention. In one strand, because of what David has done, the sword shall never depart from his house; in the other, what David has done sexually in secret, God will see to it is done in full public view, for all Israel to see (12:8–12). David's "I have sinned against the Lord" is followed immediately by Nathan's "the Lord has put away your sin" (12:13).

Where Saul was rejected as king, David retains his crown. Readers of the stories may find this unfair, but the storyteller has to deal with the realities of history. More unfair, in the eyes of many readers, is the fact that while David will live the child is to die. The episode of David's intercession and his reaction to the child's death was obviously of interest. For this reason at least, the child's fate was recorded. If the story is reflection on what had already happened, the child's death had occurred. Even as prediction, a text is written some time after the events have taken place; the child may be expected to have died.

The massive impact of this story lies in the culture that allowed, even expected, God's prophet to confront God's king with the doing of wrong. The story of the confrontation was told with approval and was preserved in Israel's traditions. For Shakespeare's Hamlet, "conscience does make cowards of us all"; for Israel's prophets, conscience makes for confrontation with its kings. Fairly or not, the child died. Probably enough, the consequences of David's behavior would have filtered down. Nevertheless, what ranks as most important is that a culture expected the prophet to confront the king and get away with it.

24. Elijah, King Ahab, and Naboth (1 Kgs 21)

The story of Naboth's vineyard is another of the great biblical examples of sacred-secular relationships in ancient Israel. It is on a par with Nathan's confrontation with King David over the king's murder of Uriah and marriage to Bathsheba.

The story is simply told. Naboth had a vineyard in the town of Jezreel, next to the palace of Ahab, king of northern Israel. Ahab wanted the land for a vegetable garden—not for the view, which probably would have been stunning, looking out from high ground over the lovely valley of Esdraelon. The king made Naboth an offer: a better vineyard in exchange or payment in cash. Naboth turned him down. The land belonged in his family ("ancestral inheritance"), and there was no way he was going to sell it.

The king went home in a sulk, went to bed, turned his face to the wall, and wouldn't eat—most unroyal behavior but, as the story unfolds, most respectable. The queen, Jezebel, a foreign princess from Phoenicia, asked what was the matter. He told her. She asked him if he understood what it meant to be king and assured him she would get the vineyard for him.

Jezebel wrote some letters to the local leaders, sealed them with Ahab's seal, arranging for the leaders of his community to have Naboth framed on a capital charge. Naboth was hauled before the elders of his town, accused by a couple of false witnesses of having "cursed God and the king," sentenced to death, and executed. The message went to Jezebel: "Naboth has been stoned; he is dead." Queen Jezebel told King Ahab: "Go, take possession of the vineyard...for Naboth is not alive, but dead."

Ahab went to the vineyard, but so did the prophet Elijah—sent by God. Relations between king and prophet were not friendly. Ahab's opening words were: "Have you found me, O my enemy?" Elijah's reply was equally unwelcoming: "Have you killed and also taken possession?... Where dogs licked up the blood of Naboth, dogs will also lick up your blood." According to the biblical text, Ahab repented and was granted a stay of execution; the dynasty collapsed under his son, Joram (see 2 Kgs 9—10).

Two things cry out to be noticed. First issue: the clash of cultures. For Ahab, however he might have expressed it, being king did not put him above the law. Royal might was limited by legal right. For Jezebel, a foreign princess, the king's word was the law; legal right was determined by royal might. What the king could get away with, the king was entitled to do. At issue is the understanding of political power: is might limited by right or is might what determines right? In the first, monarchy or governmental power is limited, by culture or law or whatever. In the second, monarchy or governmental power is despotic, limited only by the forces that oppose it. "Power grows out of the barrel of a gun"; the only limit comes from the guns. The horror of history is that armies have almost invariably been preferred to arbitration in the conduct of human affairs. As Thucydides, the Greek historian, put it a few centuries after Ahab: the strong do what they have the power to do, and the weak accept what they have to accept.

Second issue: the place of the prophet. When David murdered Uriah, God is portrayed sending Nathan; when Ahab murdered Naboth, God is portrayed sending Elijah. Much can be said about motivations, foreign influences, and the like. These portrayals of prophetic figures—Samuel who sacked Saul, Nathan who rebuked David, Elijah who condemned Ahab—helped set a model in Israel where kings were understood to be under the law (cf. Deut 17:14–20). To the best of our knowledge, kings certainly did not appreciate it. Despite the prophets, iniquitous and oppressive laws were still enacted (see Isa 10:1–4) and power-brokers still worked their will on their people (see Mic 2:1–2). For all that, something of the vision survived: royal power was not unlimited; no power is unlimited.

REFLECTIVE MOMENTS FOR PART FIVE A

How do I feel about Saul's situation? Did he get a rough deal? Was Samuel playing a pretty hard power game? What are my reactions around the claim "obedience is better than sacrifice"?

◦━

King David had a man killed and took his wife; King Ahab had a man killed and took his vineyard. Nathan confronted David; Elijah confronted Ahab. Should representatives of a culture's values confront leaders who are seen to violate those values? Does that let the fanatics loose on the politicians? Where are my feelings in all this?

◦━

Saul was condemned for failure in religious obedience. David and Ahab were condemned for secular crimes, theft and murder. Are both the religious and the secular here to be considered God's law with both equally punishable? Is the same understanding of the role of the prophet present for Samuel, Nathan, and Elijah? Are Samuel, Nathan, and Elijah portrayed acting under the same understanding of the role of the ruler? In modern society, do I want similar forces to act in their place? If so, who or what would they be?

Reflective Activity

Create a collage of stories from newspapers or magazines that reflect aspects of these biblical characters (Saul and Samuel, David and Nathan, Ahab and Elijah). What further insights emerge for you?

(B) Prophetic Truth: Confronting the Issue

25. Two Nameless Prophets at Bethel (1 Kgs 13)

This story moves from the intensely dramatic to the peacefully idyllic and back to the dramatic again. Two prophets are involved; one lies about God's word, but prophesies truthfully; the other prophesies truthfully, but disobeys God's word and dies for his disobedience. Other key figures are a king and a lion. It is an intricate story; the complexity of scholarship around it need not detain us here. Something of its intricacy is easily visible: the man of God, who disobeys and dies, prophesies accurately about the altar's future; the old prophet of Bethel, who lies about his lunch invitation, prophesies accurately about the man of God's fate and his oracle and at the same time affirms his prophetic status.

According to the story, Jeroboam—king of the newly established breakaway kingdom of northern Israel—was presiding at a ceremony of incense burning, when a man of God from Judah disrupted the liturgy, hurling an oracle against the altar. The prompt collapse of the altar and the freezing of the king's outstretched arm indicate that the man of God has clout. The king wisely invites him for a meal and a reward. The man of God declines, citing God's command not to accept hospitality but to return home by a different route. High drama indeed: a royal liturgy disrupted, an altar publicly shattered, a king's arm frozen at full stretch, and a royal honor declined.

The scene changes abruptly: lunch for two. A new figure is introduced, an old prophet who lived at Bethel. He invites the other back to lunch; when the other demurs, citing God's command, the old prophet from Bethel claims to have received the word of the Lord countermanding the order. At the end of the sentence, the text has just two

Hebrew words: he lied (13:18). As they're enjoying a pleasant lunch, the old man drops his bombshell: you have disobeyed God's command; you'll never make it to the grave of your ancestors. Lunch finished, they saddle up a donkey for the visitor and he rides off.

The scene switches back to drama. The report came in of the man of God lying dead in the road, while the lion responsible remained there and so did the donkey. Lions carry off their kill for private consumption; donkeys do not stay around as alternative provender. The "finger of God" is clear. The old prophet brought the body back, buried it in his own grave at Bethel, and enjoined his sons: bury me with him when the time comes; he is the genuine article and his words will come true.

As it stands, the text has been edited to support Josiah's reform, a couple of centuries after Jeroboam. An earlier story is likely, exploring the prophetic experience. The moral seems to be that prophets who have been in touch with God (in this case receiving both an oracle and a command) should not let themselves be deceived by others. At the same time, in this story, the prophet who is a self-confessed liar prophesies truly about both the death of the man of God and the outcome of his oracle against the altar. Prophecy may be a mysterious business; obedience to God plays a prominent role. Truth and deception are entangled here; above all, the truth of the word, the truth of the prophet, and the truth of fulfillment.

26. Micaiah ben Imlah (1 Kgs 22)

The strange experience of having prophets in the community was explored by Israel in three stories: 1 Kings 13 (with one king and two prophets); 1 Kings 22 (with two kings, two prophets, and a prophetic band of about four hundred); and Jeremiah 28 (with two prophets). We have just explored 1 Kings 13; it is time to turn to 1 Kings 22.

The first challenge to any reader is, as so often, to discern whether this is report or story; a report of an event described as it happened, or a story already distilling the meaning of the event. When the junior of the two kings (king of Judah) makes the running, we suspect a story. When the lone prophet says one thing but does another, our suspicions are strengthened. When the senior king (king of Israel) refuses the prophecy he should have wanted and demands the truth in its place, the prophecy he surely did not want, we can be certain we are dealing with a story—or a most unusual and unlikely event.

It is a rich and dense story. We can sample a few insight-giving moments. While the messenger sought Micaiah, the four hundred prophets put on a splendid liturgy with iron horns symbolizing the defeat of the foe. The discerning might notice a problem. Horns of iron do not usually lie around Israelite cities waiting for a prophet to put them to use. Realization: it was a carefully prepared liturgy and the horns were made to measure. The message was probably made to measure too. Rats! So much for spontaneity and the revelation of God's will. Some prophetic figures are not to be trusted.

Meantime, the messenger tells Micaiah what the four hundred have said and suggests he say the same. Micaiah clings to the mantra of the canonical prophets of Israel: "whatever the Lord says to me, that I will speak" (22:14). But he doesn't. He says to the king of Israel exactly what the four hundred had said (v. 15). It is the king who thunders: "tell me nothing but the truth in the name of the Lord" (v. 16). Realization: the king knew where the truth wasn't— not among his prophets.

Micaiah reveals his vision: the king dead and his army defeated (22:17). Naturally, the king does not like the idea; naturally, Micaiah fears for his life. He reveals the origin of prophetic truth: he has stood in the council of the Lord. The king of Israel was to die in battle; a spirit from God would entice him, by lying to him through his prophets (vv. 19–23). Zedekiah, head of the four hundred and therefore one of those prophets, had to protest or lose his job. He belts Micaiah on the cheek and demands to know how the spirit of the Lord had passed from him to Micaiah (v. 24). A good question. When does "the one" speak truth, and, on the contrary, when do "the many" surrender to the well-concealed allure of the good life and social status?

The king is not bothered with trifles of religious protocol and orders the troublesome Micaiah jailed until his royal return. Micaiah gets to speak one of the great exit lines in biblical literature: "if you return in peace, the Lord has not spoken by me" (v. 28).

The king of Israel arranges for the king of Judah to wear full royal robes into battle, while he (Israel) will disguise himself. The enemy is momentarily deceived but sees through the ruse. An archer fires an arrow without taking aim (literally: in his innocence—a pointer to God's guidance of the arrow) and hits the disguised king of Israel in the tiny space between "the scale armor and the breastplate" (v. 34). So the king of Israel bleeds to death at Ramoth-gilead, propped up bravely in his chariot. One up to Micaiah. The king, poor man, dies for the truth he knew but did not want to recognize. Realization: it is not easy to escape the truth one knows but wants to hide from—much less to hide from God.

27. Jeremiah and Hananiah (Jer 28)

Jeremiah 28 is the third of our stories revealing early Israel's efforts to explore the phenomenon of prophecy:

issues arose around conflict with authority, conflict between prophets themselves, and conflict between true prophecy and false. 1 Kings 13 was about a prophet's fidelity, in a context involving one king and one other prophet; 1 Kings 22 was about a king's failure, in a context involving two kings and some four hundred other prophets; Jeremiah 28 is about two prophets, in a context involving two contradictory prophecies. In such stories, Israel's thinkers explored the understanding of their experience of prophets.

The two prophets in Jeremiah 28 are Jeremiah himself and Hananiah ben Azzur. Jeremiah's message has been that God is responsible for Judah's exile, its being overwhelmed and swept up into Babylon's empire. Hananiah's message is the exact opposite, that God is deeply opposed to what is happening and will intervene in history to change it. Says Hananiah, according to the story: "in two years God will bring back what has been taken away—the temple vessels, the king, the exiles—and will restore things as they were." Says Jeremiah, according to the story: "Amen! May the Lord do so; may the Lord fulfill the words that you have prophesied. That would be nice, Hananiah, may it happen as you say; but, alas, it won't. It would need to come true before people will believe God sent you" (see vv. 6–9).

What mattered for ancient Israel were the criteria for deciding who speaks for God. It still matters for us. In this case, was it Jeremiah or Hananiah? The story's criterion is simple and commonsense: *cui bono?*—who benefits? It has Jeremiah say to Hananiah: "The prophets who preceded you and me from ancient times prophesied war, famine/woe, and pestilence against many countries and great kingdoms. As for the prophet who prophesies peace, when the word of that prophet comes true, then it will be known that the Lord has truly sent the prophet" (vv. 8–9). Predicting war, famine, and pestilence does not make a prophet popular; neither does predicting defeat. Predicting victory or peace is likely to be popular. Popularity pays.

Discerning spirits will know how to gauge what is popular and what is not. As we have seen in recent years, sometimes in certain circles messages of dire disaster are the fashion and therefore popular; in other circles, sometimes messages of love and peace are in vogue and popular. What is fashionable and in vogue is usually popular, but seldom universally. The story implies: if it's popular, it's suspect.

The Hebrew and Greek texts differ on one key point: the importance of externals. The Hebrew version has "the prophet Hananiah" and "the prophet Jeremiah." Both figures use the proper formula: "Thus says the Lord/the Lord of hosts, the God of Israel." True and false can't be told apart by externals. On the other hand, the Greek version (LXX: Jer 35:1–17) opens with "Hananiah the false prophet"; the hearers know in advance. In real life, it is not so easy. Traditional formulas do not answer anxious questions. Not even traditional common sense generates certainty. Common sense has Jeremiah say, without naming names, that a prophecy of peace will need to come true before the prophet can be accepted as from God (28:9).

Yet determining which is right can be a matter of life and death, and waiting for more evidence may not be possible. In this story, sometime later Jeremiah received the word of the Lord and that was the end of the matter. He was sent back to tell Hananiah that the Lord had not sent him and that he, Hananiah, had made the people trust in a lie. As a result, within the year he will be dead (vv. 15–16). The story ends: "In that same year…the prophet Hananiah died."

Prophecy demanded discernment of Israel and it does of us. Prophets were not to be trusted simply because they claimed to speak in God's name or manipulated all the right language. Prophets were perhaps to be trusted if what they said was not what their audience wanted to hear—perhaps. They weren't mugs in ancient Israel.

REFLECTIVE MOMENTS
FOR PART FIVE B

Israel had a number of criteria by which to judge the authenticity of prophecy: obedience, orthodoxy, fulfillment, self-interest, presence in God's court, and so on. How helpful are any of these? How do I judge among those claiming to speak for God today?

Φ

According to the stories, the "man of God" at Bethel died for his disobedience and the prophet Hananiah died for speaking what was not God's word. Micaiah ben Imlah nearly paid for his prophecy with his life. Jeremiah was saved from death by a powerful patron (Jer 26:24). Are the values of religious faith of similar importance to me—their presence giving life or their absence denying meaning?

Φ

The account of Jeremiah's conflict with Hananiah associates false prophecy with the profit motive. Generating false hope may pay better than proclaiming unpopular truth. Would I make much the same negative judgment today about religious groups and practices that pander to people's insecurity and uncertainty?

Φ

Micaiah ben Imlah claims to have stood in the court of God and listened to the views proposed there. Does that cut any ice with me? Did it cut any ice with King Ahab, who knew that the four hundred prophets did not have the truth

(1 Kgs 22:16) and went to his death in battle despite Micaiah's prophecy? Do we still do things like that?

Reflective Activity

Trust and truth are key aspects of prophecy. Take some paints, or thick colored markers (felt-tipped pens), or oil pastels (whatever you have available) and—using color, line, and shape—create something from any of these scenes that expresses trust and truth for you. Give a title and subtitle to what you have done. What insights emerge for you?

(C) PROPHETIC BOOKS: CONFRONTING THE PEOPLE

28. Headlining the Message (Amos 3)

Hebrew prophets may have fired off one-liners like modern politicians groping for sound-grabs. Given a wrongful situation, they turned up on the scene with searingly honest words, usually including a description of the wrongdoing and an announcement of the wrongdoers' fate—what Dostoevsky might have called crime and punishment.

Either the prophet or intelligent disciples, realizing that something significant was afoot, gathered groups of the one-liners (more respectfully called prophetic oracles) into collections. In due course, the collections were gathered and put together to form prophetic books. There is good evidence for it in Amos and Hosea, and there are traces of it in Isaiah; with the books of Jeremiah and Ezekiel the process appears to have been somewhat different.

A good example of how it may have worked on occasion for collections is given in Jeremiah 36. Prohibited from speaking in public, Jeremiah dictates a selection of his sayings to his secretary. Baruch, the secretary, is told on the appropriate occasion to read the sayings in public. The king—who felt much the same way about a prophet as Henry did about Becket or jumped-up dictators do about left-wing clerics—has the sayings read and burns them a few columns at a time. But it is not as easy as that. God told Jeremiah to get another scroll and dictate the sayings all over again.

A glance at the Book of Amos shows straightaway how different chapters 1—2 are from chapters 3—6, and how different chapters 7—9 are from both of them. Amos 1—2, without parallel in the Older Testament, contains highly patterned oracles fulminating against foreign cities or countries for gross injustice in war—breaches of the ancient equivalent of the Geneva convention. The collection ends with a fearful attack on (northern) Israel. Equally unparalleled is the collection in Amos 7—9. At its core are five visions, two pairs carefully patterned, and at the end the fifth, which is a shocker—the temple (probably at Bethel in the northern kingdom) is to be shattered and there will be no survivors among the people.

Amos 3—6 is a more conventional collection of oracles. We can get some feel for the literary skills of the ancient world if we read Amos 3 with the realization that it is the headline chapter for a collection, chapters 3—6.

It has a banner opening—both eye-catcher and heart-stopper at the same time—that probably neither *The Tablet* (in the United Kingdom) nor the *National Catholic Reporter* (in the United States) would want to print. Amos has Israel's God say:

> You only have I known of all the families of the earth; therefore I will punish you for all your iniquities.

No wonder prophets did not win popularity contests.

The next verses (3:3–8) form a dense little gem that says "forget popularity; this is about necessity." Cause and effect are inextricably linked. Lions roar to let the world know they have captured their prey; any earlier and the prey would take flight. Traps aren't sprung by accident. Well, the cause is out there: the lion has roared; God has spoken. The effect is obvious: people had better fear and the prophet has to prophesy. Nothing to do with popularity; it is a matter of necessity.

With these two to catch attention, the collection moves to a saying that strikes at the heart of the people (3:9–11). Gather a jury from Philistines and Egyptians, the most vicious villains available, and even they will find you guilty of violence and oppression. Your fate: to be stripped and plundered by your enemies. God says it; enemies do it.

There is more, but it is in the same vein. Serious social wrongdoing leads to serious social collapse. You can bet your God on it.

29. Patterns and the Message (Amos 7—9)

There is dual conflict here: God and Israel; prophet and priest. God and the prophet both win. In literary study, generations pore over the significance of symbolism. Shakespeare may be thought to be transparent; his symbolism is deep. T. S. Eliot may often be opaque; his symbolism too is deep. When it came to symbolism, the ancient Israelites were no slouches either. The oracles of Amos 1—2 were clear: like its neighbors, northern Israel had been found guilty of wrongdoing and sentenced (= "for three transgressions...and for four"), Israel's appeal had been denied (= "I will not revoke the punishment"), as a consequence northern Israel will be destroyed (= "flight shall perish from the swift"). The symbols of Amos 7—9 spell out the same message.

In Amos 7—9, the symbols are in the visions. The first two are transparent, with results that are benign. The second two are opaque and their interpretation malign. The less said

about the fifth the better; more than symbolic, it is grue-
some. The first two visions that Amos reports God showed
him are transparent: locusts and drought mean starvation
and death. Amos appeals: "Lord God, don't!" The appeal
succeeds; God says: "It shall not be." The third and fourth
visions are opaque: a plumb line and a basket of summer
fruit. Both builders and wreckers use plumb lines and the
basket of summer fruit is uncertain but hopeful. Until Amos
knows what the visions symbolize, appeal is out of the question. So Amos is mute. God asks what Amos sees. Amos
answers. God interprets the symbol seen; it is malign. The
plumb line is for destruction; the basket of fruit echoes
the end (a pun in Hebrew). God has shown it, but opaquely.
The prophet has named it. God has interpreted it. Appeal
does not happen. In the fifth vision, the shattered temple (of
Bethel) and the slaughtered people symbolize the destruction
and the end.

If those hearing this appalling sequence wanted to
know why such a fate was in store for them, those putting
the collection together threw in a few of Amos's oracles that
make the point. They are at the end of chapter 8 (vv. 4–14).
First the causes (vv. 4–6); then the consequences (vv. 7–14).
The causes can be summed up as injustice: trampling on the
needy, bringing ruin to the poor, putting greed before God,
practicing deceit, and exploiting the poor and needy. A society that is rotten collapses. It did in the time of the prophets;
it does now.

At the end of chapter 7, there is an anecdote. It comes
between the third and fourth visions, probably because it is
associated with Amos's proclamation of God's word against
northern Israel and its king (the high places of Isaac, the
sanctuaries of Israel, the house of Jeroboam). Amaziah,
the priest of Bethel, a royal sanctuary, sends a message to the

king telling him what Amos has been saying and the trouble such prophetic words have been causing.

Without waiting for instructions from the king, the text has the priest (Amaziah) give Amos orders to move on; he has no license to prophesy at Bethel where the king's authority holds sway. Poor Amaziah, it was a mistake; he was going one-on-one against God. Amos spells out the opposition clearly. You Amaziah say: "Never again prophesy at Bethel." God said: "Go, prophesy to my people." Not a good position to be in; a little like lying down in front of the unstoppable—a bulldozer or a tank, if you like. The consequences that Amos predicts for Amaziah and his family (wife, sons and daughters, land, himself) form probably the harshest indictment of an individual in the Bible. Authorities beware!

30. Reasons for the Message (Jer 7)

A valuable aspect of Jeremiah 7:1–15 is its density as a summary of the message of Israel's prophets. A number of details keep interpreters busy; the main thrust is what will concern us here. Particularly intriguing—and not noticed enough—is that the text does not report a speech from Jeremiah to the people but a command from God to Jeremiah: "Proclaim there this word" (7:2). The prophetic message is coming straight from the horse's mouth, from God. Surprisingly, there is no record of Jeremiah's delivering the speech. The theme recurs in another story, in Jeremiah 26, but it is a different story. Jeremiah 7 is about the message of the prophets; Jeremiah 26 is about the fate of the prophets. The two provide an excellent example of the potential of what may have been one *event* to generate two different *accounts*.

The speech is to be addressed to the "people of Judah" entering the Jerusalem temple, presumably on a feast day; it is a dense text. The proclamation is put both positively,

"Amend your ways," and negatively, "Do not trust in these deceptive words." The plea to amend assumes there is still time for it; later, after verse 12, the time for amendment has passed. Many argue that two independent passages have been combined. If so, the combination is eminently understandable; two stages are indicated.

The principal focus of the "sermon" is on the behaviors that are to be amended and the deceptive words that are not to be trusted. The two are stated globally in verses 3–4. The behaviors (v. 3) are taken up in verses 5–7; the deceptive words (v. 4) are unpacked in verses 8–10. In both cases, the issues are identical: social injustice and religious infidelity. In verses 5–7, the issue of social injustice is given particular emphasis; if anything, in verses 8–10, religious infidelity is given rather more space.

Amendment (vv. 5–7) is articulated first in terms of social justice: "if you truly act justly with one another." This is spelled out in the traditional triad of the defenseless—the alien, the orphan, and the widow. To this is added Jeremiah's particular concern over the "shedding of innocent blood in this place" (the land or the temple). Religious infidelity is listed second, going after other gods, with the particular focus of "to your own hurt." Religious infidelity may not damage God; it certainly damages Israel.

The "destructive words" come next (vv. 8–10). First, categories of social injustice: stealing, murder, adultery, dishonesty; second, religious infidelity: making offerings to Baal and going after "other gods that you have not known." The reasons for the great attraction that the worship of Baal exercised on Israel are unknown to us. Apparently, early in Israel's story, it did not seem to be a problem; King Saul gave two of his sons names with the god-element Baal (Ishbaal and Meribaal). Later, the worship of Baal became an enormous problem to Israel—perhaps much as practical atheism is to so many of us today. "Other gods you have not known" may point to the attraction of novelty. The familiar easily becomes boring; Israel was surely familiar with its God.

Whatever we make of Israel's motives, the outcome was clear. Social injustice and religious infidelity made Israel incompatible with God. As northern Israel had lost its freedom to the Assyrians in 722 (the northern exile), so Judah would lose its freedom to the Babylonians in 587 (the exile). From Jeremiah, the word was devastating: "I will cast you out of my sight" (7:15).

31. Names Are the Message (Hos 1)

The presence of three collections of sayings in the Book of Hosea is easy enough to see. Chapters 1—3 concern the symbolism of Hosea's married life. Just as the two totally different collections in Amos 1—2 and 7—9 are both unique in the Bible, so too is Hosea 1—3; there is nothing comparable elsewhere in the Bible. The collection begins with divorce between God and Israel and ends with reconciliation. Despite the reconciliation, chapter 4 levels an indictment against Israel and what follows continues in a similar vein; chapter 11 returns to images of a loving God. It is language of God at the Bible's best: "it was I who taught Ephraim [= northern Israel] to walk, I took them up in my arms....I led them with cords of human kindness, with bands of love." Chapters 4—11 make sense as a second collection. A third collection is signaled when chapter 12 ignores the change and returns to the indictment; chapter 14 in due course returns to gratuitous reconciliation, "I will heal their disloyalty; I will love them freely" (14:4). The probable collections are Hosea 1—3, 4—11, and 12—14.

Hosea 1 is not for the squeamish. Oceans of ink have been poured out trying to clean it up, claiming for example that it was all Hosea's idea. As a matter of fact, according to the text it wasn't; it is proclaimed as God's will. If we can get over being squeamish, this chapter, along with chapter 3, gives one of the Bible's best theology lessons: we are loved, miserable rotters though we may sometimes be. Well, Israel sometimes was. So there is hope for us.

It all begins with a third-person report about Hosea. "When the Lord first spoke through Hosea" (v. 2). "First" tells us the writer is aware of a "second"; the second time may be different from the first. We are entitled to hope.

The text says God told Hosea to marry a prostitute and have children with her. The pious say Hosea thought this up when his marriage went on the rocks; the text says that God ordered it. God gives a reason for it too. Israel is behaving like a prostitute in abandoning all sense of fidelity to its God. God's command makes Hosea a symbol of Israel. There will be a happy ending, but it is slow in coming.

God intervenes three more times, giving the prophet a name for each one of the three children. The names are definitely bad news: Jezreel (inviting three puns, all of them unpleasant), Not-pitied (no pun needed), and Not-my-people. The third one is the climax: Not-my-people. The best thing that the people of Israel had going for them was the belief that they were God's people. Here the prophet claims that God told him to name his child Not-my-people, because Israel wasn't God's people anymore. These are not your ordinary, everyday children; these are a prophet's children. For people of faith, this is a very scary situation.

After verse 9, the next three verses reverse the situation immediately (different translations number the verses differently). Instead of the ill-omened name Jezreel, it will be "children of the living God." For Not-pitied, the lovely name Ruhamah, Pitied; for Not-my-people, a name to rejoice in, Ammi, My-people. (The Roman Catholic lectionary stops at v. 9, a choice by the lectionary that even benignly interpreted is most unfortunate. One may hope it was benign; not anti-Semitic, simply unfortunate.)

The marital reconciliation theme is spelled out again in chapter 3 without reference to the children. This time, it is a first-person report, "the Lord said to *me* again." Hosea is to love an adulteress; we presume it was the same woman from chapter 1, who had walked out on him. Once again, it is the reason God gives that matters: "just as the Lord loves the people of Israel, though they turn to other gods" (3:1). We can love those who do wrong; according to Hosea, so does God. To simplify the language of Hosea 3:1, "I [God] love the people of Israel, even though they don't love me."

My dear Saint Paul, you've been beaten to the punch by a mere eight centuries or so. We believe we are loved by our God, sinners though we are. What joy!

32. God and Love for Israel (Hos 11)

Hosea 11 is one of the most powerful expressions of God's love to be found in the Bible. Mind you, we don't expect lovers to be logical. There is a bit of a problem lurking in the chapter, but in our wisdom we will let the love overwhelm it.

Hosea has the text as a soliloquy, God talking. "When Israel was a child, I loved him, and out of Egypt I called my son" (11:1). God's love comes first, then God's action. Unfortunately, Israel's response was much like ours: "The more I called them, the more they went from me" (v. 2).

The picture of God's behavior is incredible, coming from a biblical prophet (although the Hebrew text has its difficulties; see especially vv. 3–5). I, God, taught them to walk (Israel as toddler), I picked them up in my arms (Israel as infant), I treated them with love, like parents who lift their children to their cheeks (God as nurturing parent); "I bent down to them and fed them" (v. 4). It is hard to imagine a more parentally loving image of God. We need to hear the passion, see the love.

We need to hear it, because there is a flip side to it. Like us, the more they were loved, the further from God they went. Says God, according to Hosea: "They have refused to return to me" (v. 5). So the whole thing is off; back they are to go to where they came from. "They shall return to the land of Egypt." Understandable enough; logical enough.

But love is not logical, not even God's love. Hosea puts the words in God's mouth: "How can I give you up...? How can I hand you over...? My heart recoils within me; my compassion grows warm and tender" (v. 8). The divorce is off. The commitment is on. The reason is made clear: "For I am God...the Holy One in your midst" (9). Forget logic. Forget the human need for a predictable God who follows the rules. Hosea, God love the man, is talking as a prophet to Israel of a God who loves and loves passionately.

We do not *know* that Hosea was right; we *believe*. Just as we do not *know,* at least initially, that those who appear to love us are not impelled by largely unconscious imperatives—or we for them. We *believe* in love. We live out of it. We do not have logical certainty; in that sense, we do not know. Testing love is about the same as denying love. So we believe we are loved by those who love us. Hosea, Isaiah, and many others dare to make the claim that God loved Israel. Their words invite us to the belief that we too are loved, that God loves us. It is tricky using a word like love to speak of God's relationship with us. It sounds a bit soft and woolly. On the other hand, the Older Testament uses it and the Newer Testament uses it, so maybe we can run the risk of using it too. We can always play safe and speak of God's commitment or God's fidelity, and so on. That may leave us more at ease, but it has us backing off the language of the Bible. To be brutally realistic about it, some of the behavior attributed to God is illogical enough that only the language of love is appropriate. We may as well be at ease with it. We may as well accept the possibility that God sees more deeply than we do and, as a result, loves more deeply than we do.

It is an extraordinary faith that claimed God's love for Israel, because the life of Israel at the time of the prophets was no rose garden. Hosea's nation was overrun by the Assyrians. Isaiah's beloved Jerusalem was taken by the Babylonians. But God loved them; how then did it happen? It does happen. It happened then; it happens now. Appalling things happen, far away (in foreign countries) and near at hand (across the street). Hosea, Isaiah, and many others knew that and they still believed in God's love. We are invited to do the same and still believe in God's love. How much easier it would be if it was all clear and logical. But then, if it was logical, it wouldn't be love.

There is no trace of calculation here. We might be theologically rash to speak of God being swept away by the overwhelming power of passion. If we did, we would scarcely mean sexual passion; but there is more, much more, to love than sexual passion. We humans are capable of such love; should we dare think it beyond God's reach? Should we think it below God's divinity? Certainly the biblical text gives the impression of a God swept away by overwhelming love for us. What does God see that we don't dare to see?

"I am God and no mortal." Forget logic; can you believe it, I God am in love.

33. God and Life (Jer 2)

The God of Israel is often referred to as a "jealous God." For most of us, jealousy is an ugly emotion; we may feel it, but we tend to be ashamed of it. So we tend to find language of a "jealous God" ugly, shameful, and off-putting. It is important to realize what lies behind this sort of language, to realize what it meant (and means) to go after "other gods." As Jeremiah has God say: "they went far from me, and went after worthless things, and became worthless themselves" (Jer 2:5). Don't we all?

I know of no passage in the Bible quite so passionate and so eloquent about the implications of abandoning faith in God. We can listen. We can steep ourselves in it.

One image sticks with me and will not let me go. "My people," says God, "have forsaken me, the fountain of living waters; and dug out cisterns for themselves, cracked cisterns that can hold no water" (2:13). "My people"; updated, that is "us." Of course Jeremiah was thundering about Israel, but today it is us, wherever we are. The image: cracked cisterns, leaky cisterns that hold no water.

At heart, I'm a farm boy. Every farmer knows the need for water. Drought and empty water storage spell death; water by the bucketful spells life. Every gardener knows that without water almost nothing grows. In Israel, under the burning midsummer sun, I rode my motorbike around a corner and there was an oasis (Tirzah), verdant luxuriant green in the midst of the barren lifeless dry. The image sticks with me.

Jeremiah has God say: "they have forsaken me the fountain of living water, and dug out cisterns for themselves, cracked cisterns that can hold no water" (2:13). If faith is not life-giving, there is something wrong with faith. If living water does not produce luxuriant growth, something is wrong. It may be the soil; it may be the quality of the water. But something's wrong.

John's Gospel has Jesus, standing in the Temple on the last and greatest day of the festival, take up the image: "Let the one who believes in me drink....Out of the believer's heart shall flow rivers of living water" (John 7:38). Ezekiel develops the same image: a river, flowing out from the Temple, growing mightier and mightier, producing unbelievable fertility, growth, and life (Ezek 47:1–12). It has been said that it would be easier to believe in the resurrection of Christ if only Christians had risen faces? If faith is not life-giving, there is something wrong with faith.

What gets Jeremiah mad is the quality of the God that Israel can abandon. "Has a nation changed its gods, even though they are no gods? But my people have changed their glory for something that does not profit" (2:11). What gets me mad is the capacity of people to distort the quality of Christian faith—deprive it of life; kill it!

Jeremiah speaks with the great thinkers of ancient Israel when he says that if we go after worthless things we become worthless ourselves. "Vanity they pursued, vanity they became" (2:5, *Jerusalem Bible*). Leaders, synagogues and churches, can help unfold the meaning of faith. Ultimately though, we do it for ourselves—and God help us if we get it wrong. No wonder Israel got its knickers in a knot over the ease with which people abandon God.

One of the fantastic insights Jeremiah ties into this chapter is the association of faith with freedom. Living water grows one free. "Is Israel then a slave...to be preyed on like this?" (2:14). "Preyed on like this"; it's your own fault, says Jeremiah: "Have you not brought this upon yourself by forsaking the Lord your God?" (2:17). Lord, let me believe; let there be living water and let it give me life and make me free.

34. God and Justice (Isa 5)

It is important for us to see how the prophet portrays God reacting to the injustice seen as rampant in society. Equally important is to see how a general statement in the prophet's song is illustrated by a series of concrete examples of injustice among the people of Israel.

Seven sayings of judgment, introduced with a cry of pain ("Woe" or "Ah") follow Isaiah's song (Isa 5:8, 11, 18,

20, 21, 22; 10:1). In addition, there are five refrains that end other sayings (identifiable by reference to God's anger and God's hand outstretched to strike; Isa 5:25; 9:12, 17, 21; 10:4). The combination (with six sayings of judgment from chapter 5 and one from chapter 10; and one refrain from chapter 5 and four from chapters 9—10) suggests the presence of collections of sayings here that extend either side of Isaiah 6:1—9:7, as a central and independent collection of its own. Sections of Israel's prophetic books may have grown out of such collections. The complexity is considerable; interpretation is uncertain and hypothetical. As with Judges 2—8, it is important for us to be aware of the insight, intelligence, and intensity at work in ancient Israel. We do not always need to be sure about the process in order to profit from the product, the biblical text we have.

The song itself (Isa 5:1–7) begins with a love song for the beloved: "Let me sing for my beloved my love-song concerning his vineyard" (v. 1). For once, it sounds as if a prophet is to be a source of joy rather than a proclaimer of disaster. The first sour note comes with the expectation; the beloved expected grapes and the vineyard produced wild grapes (v. 3). Suddenly we find ourselves in a court scene, judging between owner and vineyard. The next shock is to discover that the owner claims to be able to "command the clouds that they rain no rain upon it" (v. 6). Only God can do that. In which case, is God the owner and are we the vineyard?

Verse 7 spells it out clearly. The vineyard is Israel and Judah. God expected justice and instead got bloodshed from the vineyard; God expected righteousness and instead heard a cry, the cry of the oppressed. The wordplay is powerful: justice *(mishpat)* and bloodshed *(mishpach);* righteousness *(tsedaqah)* and cry *(tse'aqah).*

The crimes that exemplify this bloodshed and oppression are worth our noting. There are in fact seven of them;

six here and one in chapter 10. The first crime is the expropriation of property (taking people's land); defeat will leave the land empty and desolate (5:8–10). The second is the pursuit of pleasure that leads to loss of faith; its consequence is exile without faith (5:11–13). Military defeat and being driven into exile were well-known in the ancient Near East. Little has changed today.

The third of the crimes is aggressive evil and cynical skepticism (5:18–19). The fourth denounces a total reversal of values, calling evil good and good evil, bitter sweet and sweet bitter (5:20). The fifth denounces the self-interest and self-centeredness that is not open to the judgment of society and the law (5:21). The sixth pillories the good life when it is associated with bribery and corruption (5:22).

In chapter 10, the climactic seventh evil points to a level of criminality that is endemic and reaching to the highest levels of society (10:1–4). The laws made are evil and oppressive. Justice is denied the needy; the poor are robbed of their right. As the prophet Micah puts it: the powerful lie awake all night figuring how to fiddle the law and then they do it, because they have the power to (Mic 2:1–2). Might is right and the law can be a tool of might. Isaiah invokes the weak as the criterion. Widow and orphan are spoil and prey; the powerless are powerless. In Isaiah's eyes, the outcome will be social collapse, defeat, and disaster (10:3).

Ultimately, social corruption destroys society. Where will help come from? Where will wealth be safe? Which is better: crouching among the prisoners or falling among the slain? Empires rise and fall slowly. Without justice, they fall surely.

35. The Fate of the Prophets (Jer 26)

Jeremiah 7 and 26 offer us an understanding of the prophetic role that is beyond price. They probably incorporate insights from Israel's more general experience of the prophets; we have them now in the book of the prophet Jeremiah, as help to our understanding of these mighty figures.

As we have seen, Jeremiah 7 deals with the essence of the prophetic message: in the absence of social justice and appropriate religious fidelity, a nation is doomed—to be destroyed or to self-destruct. Jeremiah 26 takes a different tack and looks at the prophetic function, the social situation addressed by the prophet, and the reception given the prophet by society.

In both passages, the word comes directly from God; the text does not portray for us Jeremiah proclaiming it. In Jeremiah 26, however, the text does include the response of priests, prophets, and people, who "heard Jeremiah speaking these words in the house of the Lord" (26:7). So they were proclaimed.

What is important for us as readers of the Bible is to recognize how two different presentations can stem from what was probably one event. In Jeremiah 7, it is the prophetic message; in Jeremiah 26, it is the prophetic fate.

The date is given: the start of a king's reign, the reign of Jehoiakim son of Josiah. Josiah, king of Judah, had been a backer of religious reform. Would Jehoiakim follow in his father's footsteps or yield to the political and social pressures that brought about religious infidelity? With the balance of power shifting between Assyria and Babylon, the big powers of the time in that region, much was at stake for Israel. Under Josiah, a change of heart had happened; under him religious reform (deuteronomic, because based on Deuteronomy) had been begun. The issue at stake for Israel: would King Jehoiakim demonstrate fidelity to the reform and continue it?

The self-understanding of the prophet is latent in the first paragraph. What God will speak to the prophet, the prophet will speak to the people—not a word will be held back. In Jeremiah's call narrative, the same understanding is present (see Jer 1:7). The implication is clear: prophets were unpopular, and what they said could be dismissed as not from God.

In the light of this, Jeremiah's self-defense in verses 12–15 is remarkable. The death penalty is demanded because he has spoken against the temple and the city (vv. 9, 11). Jeremiah could have pointed to the evil in the city (v. 3); it was evident enough. He could have pointed to the law that was being violated (v. 4); it was clear enough. He could have appealed to the words of other prophets sent by God (v. 5); their message was the same. Jeremiah did none of these; his defense: God sent me to deliver this prophecy. It is the one thing he cannot prove. The last word given him in his summing up: "Only know for certain that if you put me to death, you will be bringing innocent blood upon yourselves...for in truth the Lord sent me to you to speak all these words in your ears" (v. 15). The discernment is left to the hearers—and to us.

One last aspect is worth notice. Priests, prophets, and people are portrayed hearing Jeremiah and laying hold of him. The royal officials arrive (v. 10). The priests and prophets make the accusation to royal officials and people (v. 11) who, after hearing Jeremiah's defense, argue in Jeremiah's favor. The text brings up two cases: on one side, Micah of Moresheth whose words against Jerusalem were taken to heart by King Hezekiah, with favorable results; on the other, Uriah of Kiriath-jearim whose words were like those of Jeremiah and whom King Jehoiakim dragged back from refuge in Egypt and had killed. Nothing is said about Jehoiakim's behavior in Jeremiah's case. At the end of the chapter, a powerful political figure, Ahikam ben Shaphan, intervenes as Jeremiah's protector and saves him from being handed over to the people. Just what was going on and what strings were being pulled we do not know.

36. The Books of the Prophets (Jer 36)

Jeremiah 36 is one of those marvelous stories that touches base in a number of places. In Jeremiah 26, the prophet is there and the king isn't; in Jeremiah 36, the king is there and the prophet isn't—but his word is. In 2 Kings 22, the word of God is heard by King Josiah; in Jeremiah 36, the word of God is burned by King Jehoiakim.

Jeremiah 36 is a story, but one that throws light on the origin and nature of prophetic books. It is when he has been gagged that Jeremiah turns to the written word: "I am prevented from entering the house of the Lord...you shall read the words...written at my dictation" (Jer 36:5–6). Hosea and Amos worked in the northern kingdom of Israel, shortly before the Assyrians closed it down in 722 BCE, putting an end to the possibility of their speaking. At one stage at least in his career, Isaiah's prophecy dried up; the Lord is "hiding his face from the house of Jacob" (Isa 8:17). He turned to a document ("testimony") and his followers; "Bind up the testimony, seal the teaching among my disciples" (8:16). When the prophet can no longer be on the scene, the written word can still be there.

Jeremiah's document selected words from the time of two kings, Josiah (ca. 640–609) and Jehoiakim (609–598). It had to be short enough that reading it in a single royal audience could be plausible. It pulled together enough of Jeremiah's utterances that the hope could be expressed that "all of them [in Judah] may turn from their evil ways" (Jer 36:3), so that God may forgive their iniquity and their sin. Normally, Israel's prophets did not explicitly call for repentance, but it was always there as a possibility (cf. Book of Jonah), and the impact of multiple prophetic sayings, grouped in a single collection, made that possibility the more likely.

As we've seen, the Book of Hosea probably combines three such collections (chapters 1—3, 4—11, and 12—14); the

Book of Amos also has three (chapters 1—2, 3—6, and 7—9). Others are more complicated. Of course, within the Book of Isaiah we have at least a preexilic, exilic, and postexilic threesome (roughly and incompletely associated with chapters 1–39, 40–55, 56–66; "a single literary work…written over the course of some four centuries" [Marvin Sweeney]). Early in the piece, a collection comprising Isaiah 6:1—9:7 is likely, centering around the threat to Judah from Northern Israel and Syria. Surrounding it, another collection appears to begin with the Song of the Vineyard (5:1–7) and end with a fearful oracle against unjust rulers (10:1–4). It brings home to us that prophets did not write books; they went out in the streets and said what had to be said. For the most part, their disciples did the writing. In Jeremiah 36, it is Baruch; in Hosea 3, it is Hosea himself ("the Lord said to me again"), but in Hosea 1 it is another ("the Lord said to Hosea").

As we noted when looking at Amos 3—and as we have just seen—there is good evidence for collections of sayings as stages on the way to prophetic books in the case of Amos and Hosea, with traces of it for Isaiah; "with the books of Jeremiah and Ezekiel the process appears to have been somewhat different." While that is true for the books of these two prophets, it is ironic that a single chapter in Jeremiah (chapter 36) provides as good an illustration as we could ask for as to how some of the sayings of a prophet could have been collected in a document, and how such collections might have functioned when the prophet could no longer be present in person.

In this case, Jeremiah's collected sayings had enough bite to them that, when Baruch read them in the temple, the royal officials who heard demanded a private reading; heard again, they were taken to King Jehoiakim, who adopted the standard ploy of the practical politician confronted with prophetic proclamation: bury it. In this case, he burned the scroll, piece by piece (36:23). We needn't feel superior; none of us has clean hands. It didn't do the king much good either; Jeremiah was told to dictate it all again (36:28), which he did (36:32). He added a special word for King Jehoiakim: "...and his dead body shall be cast out to the heat by day and the frost by night..." (36:30–31).

A single document seldom exhausts what needs to be said. The Gospel of John notes that Jesus did "many other signs" (John 20:30). Jeremiah 36 notes that in the rewriting "many similar words were added" (36:32). Unlike the person, the word lives on.

REFLECTIVE MOMENTS
FOR PART FIVE C

What has been my idea of a prophet? Someone who spoke of the future? Someone who was scathing about what was wrong with the present? How would I feel about having one live next door? How do I react to the recent prophets I know of in our society?

*

I hear the prophets read often enough in liturgy. What do I think of their writings and their books? When I'm utterly honest, how much intelligence, gifted organization, and skilled editing do I expect to find in a prophetic book?

*

Israel's prophets spoke to a people where they judged God was abandoned and injustice was abundant. Two things for each of us to think about. First, God was abandoned: where am I in terms of faith? Have I given up on God and let myself down into the bargain? Second, injustice was abundant: to what extent do I contribute to the injustice of our society today? To what extent am I working to make my world more just? Do I think it matters to God? Does it matter to me?

❧

In my own thinking about Israel's prophets, do I understand them proclaiming as punishment what God was shortly to do to Israel? Or do I understand them pointing to the consequences of what Israel was doing to itself—with social injustice destroying the cohesion of the community and eroding Israel's military morale, and with religious infidelity abandoning the values that kept Israel alive as a society? Where are we today in faith?

❧

In more than one place, the prophets speak of God's love for us. Hosea: as I love the people of Israel even though they don't love me (3:1). Jeremiah: our honeymoon together, "your love as a bride" (2:1). Isaiah: you mean so much to me, "you are precious in my sight, and honored, and I love you" (43:4). Do I believe that for myself? Or do I view myself as unlovable? Do I believe it is beyond God to love me?

Reflective Activity

What is a central message that stays with me from the prophets? Where is that message reflected in my life? What feelings does the message evoke?

Use color, line, and shape to image these feelings. Give the image a title and subtitle. What stance toward yourself does the title invite you to take?

PART SIX:
Beyond the Past

THE FUTURE

Introduction

All the preexilic prophetic books speak of hope and the future to come after the prophesied catastrophes. Apart from radical Christian reinterpretation in the person of Jesus Christ, these prophecies have remained largely unfulfilled. The irony is patent: the prophecies of catastrophe have been fulfilled to the letter; the prophecies of salvation have not.

One way of coping with this is to focus on the understanding of God expressed in the prophecies of salvation, rather than on the particular form described for the future. In this way, some of the loveliest and much-quoted passages of the Older Testament can continue to fuel faith. Beyond the whimsy, the wishful thinking, and sometimes the downright materialism of the portrayal of the promised future (for materialism, see Isa 60:5–7, 11–16), the focus of faith can be on the prophets' understanding of the benevolence of their God. Perhaps the loveliest is given God in Hosea: "I love them, even if they don't love me" (loose but accurate translation of Hos 3:1). Perhaps the saddest is to be found both early and late in the Book of Isaiah: "They will not hurt or destroy on all my holy mountain" (11:9; 65:25); alas, they have done little else but hurt and destroy on that holy mountain ever since.

The four passages here touch on faith in God. Such faith can be life-giving (Ezek 37); it can be hugely fruitful (Ezek 47). Israel's faith in a God gracious and merciful, slow to anger, abounding in steadfast love, and ready to relent from punishing can give grounds for hope (Book of Jonah); the honesty of faith that can be found in Israel enables us to cope with life, confronted with the enigma of a suffering world and a loving God (Book of Job).

37. Death and New Life (Ezek 37)

The message is magnificent: the nation may be in its grave; nevertheless, it will live. The vision is spine-chilling: the bleached bones filling a valley floor begin to move, rattle, assemble, and take shape—a vast death-defying multitude. As a vision, visually it is monstrous. As a message, spiritually it is magnificent—it gives hope and promises life. Says God through the prophet: "I am going to open your graves, O my people; I will put my spirit within you, and you shall live" (37:12–14).

We need to start with Israel's image of itself. "Our bones are dried up, and our hope is lost; we are cut off completely" (37:11). It is an image that many of us have known in moments of failure and despair. It is an image that Christian pessimists suffer under today about their church.

God's word comes to Ezekiel as a vision: before it can be understood, it must be seen at least imaginatively and in the seeing experienced. The seeing begins for us with the imagination of exile, which for Israel meant defeat, departure from all that was familiar, despair of all that was hoped for. It was ugly, frightening, devastating. Ezekiel starts in the utter ignorance of faith: "O Lord God, you know" (37:3). Faith goes hand-in-hand with trust. Ezekiel is with the community of Israel exiled in a foreign country. Faith and trust are not easy when your world has collapsed around you.

In his experience of God—"the hand of the Lord came upon me"—Ezekiel is given a job to do. "Prophesy to these bones and say...." The details are given in the text; the invitation to our imaginations is there. A valley full of bones, a noise, a rattling, bones moving around finding the right bones to link up with, the coming of sinews, flesh, and skin. The full wizardry of the modern computer and the special effects of a sci-fi film would fill a screen magnificently. Imagine the horror of the moving bones and the emerging bodies and, still, the lifelessness of it all. There is no breath!

Ezekiel gets the culminating command: "Prophesy to the breath" and say "Thus says the Lord God: Come from the four winds, O breath, and breathe upon these slain, that they may live" (37:9). God's promise: "I am going to open your graves, and bring you up from your graves, O my people; and I will bring you back to the land of Israel" (37:12).

The community of exiled Israel was enabled to return to the land of Israel. Alas, the return fell far short of the hopes it raised (see Ezra 3:12). A free and independent Israel did not exist until modern times. Christian hopes were shattered by the crucifixion of Jesus; they were restored by faith in Jesus' resurrection. Jewish hopes were tortured in the pogroms and shattered by the Holocaust. For many Jews of religious faith, I fear that only Ezekiel's ignorance holds true: "O Lord God, you know." The unfolding of that, in the first instance at least, is a task begun by Jewish theologians. First and foremost, Christian faith finds itself in mute sorrow before the pain of those God loves.

Ezekiel's vision has its own meaning for Christians. It is not merely transmuted into the resurrection of Jesus. It is to be felt in the lives of individuals; it is to be hoped for in the life of the church. Obviously, it is not "I will bring you back to the land of Israel"; however, it is "you shall live" (37:5, 14). Today, as then, we live by faith and we live in trust.

Promises can focus on all-too-material things (for example, Old Testament: peace and prosperity [e.g., Isaiah], independence and land [e.g., Ezekiel]; New Testament: answers to prayer, second coming of Christ); such material hopes are often disappointed. Perhaps God works better through persons.

38. Flowing Water and New Life (Ezek 47)

It is remarkable that Amos, the first of the classical prophets, has a series of five visions at the end of his book (Amos 7—9) and Ezekiel, the last of these major prophets, has an unsurpassed cluster of visions too. Five moments are highly significant: the two big visions, God's departure from the Jerusalem temple (Ezek 8—11) and God's return, coupled with the visionary design of a new temple in Jerusalem and issues associated with it (Ezek 40—46); a little earlier is the vision of the "dry bones" (Ezek 37:1–14) and immediately after the vision of God's return to the new temple is the vision of the great river (Ezek 47:1–12). After that, there is the word of the Lord about the new and totally artificial boundaries for the tribes within Israel (Ezek 47:13—48:29). Ezekiel is a visionary and the passages each contain their message.

The message of the vision of the great river rings loud and clear, then and now: faith brings life. The river rises in the restored temple, focus of Israel's faith. It flows from below the front entrance, flowing southeast. Like any good river, it gets deeper as it goes on, ankle-deep at the start (v. 3) and soon enough too deep to cross (v. 5). Faith is similar; it gets deeper as it goes on.

The river flows through some of the most desolately barren and infertile land open to regular experience in Israel. It flows southeast from Jerusalem, through the Arabah, and into the Dead Sea (v. 8). Parts of Israel's Negev have the utter barrenness we associate with a moonscape; the savagely mountainous territory between Jerusalem and the Dead Sea is no better. Riven by deep wadis, with mountainsides that are rocky and frighteningly steep, utterly devoid of vegetation, it is as it looks: dangerous and dead.

The river brings life that is unbelievably rich. Animal life is there in plenty and fish abound (vv. 9–10). When this river enters the Dead Sea, the sea's intense saltwater becomes fresh (v. 8). "Everything will live where the river goes" (v. 9). On the banks, on both sides, all kinds of fruit-bearing trees will grow, providing fresh food every month, "because the water for them flows from the sanctuary" (v. 12).

The average farmer gets a crop once a year. As a rule, fruit-picking happens once a year. Ezekiel and all Israel knew this; the farmers and fruit-growers among us know this. Ezekiel's vision—"fresh fruit every month"—is unbelievable. It must have been for him; it certainly is for us. Unbelievable, except for that phrase at the end: "because the water for them flows from the sanctuary" (v. 12). "Their fruit will be for food, and their leaves for healing." Impossible! Yes, but true, "because the water for them flows from the sanctuary."

Food and healing; faith can give both. There is a saying: when you are in love, everything changes and nothing changes. When we have faith in God and God's love for us, everything changes and nothing changes. Ezekiel and all Israel, farmers and fruit-growers know that "fresh fruit every month" has never happened and never will. With deep faith, nothing changes—but everything does! When we are loved, we still get up in the morning, eat our meals, do our work, and go to bed at night. But from meaninglessness, isolation, and loneliness, everything has changed. When in faith we believe ourselves loved by God everything has changed— meaninglessness, isolation, loneliness. Where faith cramps our living, probably something is wrong with faith. Like Ezekiel's river, our faith should flow and give us life, abundant life.

39. Hope and Jonah (Book of Jonah)

Parables have one point; good stories may have many meanings. Jonah is a good story—a legendary prophetic story. Among the many meanings: prophets had to speak; it was no good trying to run from God; God was concerned to punish wrongdoing; God was concerned for a city like Nineveh; God could be counted on to relent from punishing. The text gives us no hook to hang a single message on, excluding others. God's grace angers Jonah. God defends the act of grace. The text leaves Jonah's reply open.

We know Israel took a pounding from its prophets proclaiming God's punishment. We know that some of its theologians claimed individuals or institutions had not been adequately reformed. We know Israel's fate in all the agony of the Babylonian exile. We do not know enough about the Book of Jonah, when and where it was put together, to know whether it could have brought a degree of comfort to ancient Israel's pain, illustrating the immensity of God's mercy and compassion. What we do know is the value for us in exploring the impact of this story on us.

Jonah's run for Tarshish is great storytelling. God said "Go east"; Jonah booked a ticket to go west; God got him. The story is very good to the sailors, who tried so hard to save Jonah's life before finally throwing him overboard. The telling of the Ninevite experience is revealing of a stratified perception. The ordinary people are portrayed knowing what has to be done and doing it; they repented (believed God and proclaimed a fast). The privilege of articulating the theology is given the king of Nineveh: "Who knows? God may repent and change his mind" (3:9). God is concerned for Nineveh (4:11).

Jonah's run for Tarshish is blocked. The text gives Jonah a song of thanksgiving to the God who has saved his life; an expression of anger at the God who has blocked his escape might have suited better; in its context the psalm is overly pious. "Deliverance belongs to the Lord!" Deliverance is granted Jonah, who is grateful. Deliverance is granted Nineveh; Jonah is displeased. We cannot be sure where the story left Israel. Where does the story leave us? Should wrongdoing always be punished? Does forgiveness always prevail? Does human society require that wrongs be righted? Where do we see God in all this?

My heart goes out to poor Jonah; he really has been shortchanged. At best, he is given half a prophetic message; it might be considered only a third of one or less. His message: "Forty days more, and Nineveh shall be overthrown" (3:4). Oddly, the text is silent about this being the word of the Lord and silent about Nineveh's wrongdoing (reported earlier in 1:2). Wrongdoing calls for repentance; in Jonah's proclamation, however, there is no call to repentance. Justice requires that wickedness be punished; in the Book of Jonah, Nineveh is not punished.

The people of Nineveh are portrayed as smart enough to know where the message came from. "The people of Nineveh believed God" (3:5a). The people of Nineveh are portrayed as smart enough to know that repentance was always a possibility. "They proclaimed a fast, and...put on sackcloth" (3:5b). Naturally, as a result, "God changed his mind" (3:10).

That is the point in the story where Jonah blows a gasket. He had proclaimed God's message: "Forty days more, and Nineveh shall be overthrown" (3:4). Alas for Jonah,

"God changed his mind" (3:10). When Jonah realized this, "he became angry" (4:1).

"O Lord! Is not this what I said while I was still in my own country? That is why I fled to Tarshish at the beginning; for I knew that you are a gracious God and merciful, slow to anger, and abounding in steadfast love and ready to relent from punishing" (4:2).

It is all there, except Jonah's final "Dammit!" And that's there too, but more politely: "And now, O Lord, please take my life from me, for it is better for me to die than to live" (4:3). The text does not give a reason for this death wish. Perhaps, for Jonah, life had no meaning when the God who inspired prophets to announce punishment could be counted on to annul it. When disorder moves to chaos, does life become unbearable?

The people of Nineveh, "everyone, great and small," confirmed by their king, knew that repentance was possible. As the king of Nineveh said: "Who knows? God may relent and change his mind; he may turn from his fierce anger, so that we do not perish" (3:9).

The point would not have been lost on those pained in Israel. Available to Nineveh, God's mercy and compassion were available to Israel, as they are to us. Jonah was angry about God's exercise of mercy, angry enough to repeat his death wish. God's defense appears unanswerable (4:7–11). The story of Jonah attempts no answer, leaving the issue open. In the story, one thing at least is certain: God's gracious mercy, hallowed in Israel's tradition, was available to Nineveh. As stories go, it is brilliant.

(What Jonah is given to say, in the intensity of his anger, is remarkable for its understanding of Israel's tradition, drawing widely on what we now have as Israel's Bible [*gracious and merciful*: Joel 2:13; Pss 111:4; 112:4; 145:8; Neh 9:17, 31; 2 Chron 30:9. Cf. Exod 34:6; Pss 86:15; 103:8;

slow to anger: Exod 34:6; Num 14:18; Joel 2:13; Pss 103:8; 145:8; Neh 9:17; *abounding in steadfast love:* Exod 34:6; Num 14:18; Joel 2:13; Pss 86:5, 15; 103:8; Neh 9:17; *ready to relent from punishing:* Exod 32:12, 14; 2 Sam 24:16; Jer 18:8; 26:3, 13, 19; 42:10; Joel 2:13; 1 Chron 21:15]).

40. Life and Job (Book of Job)

The Book of Job is legendary as a study in human suffering before God. It deals with two questions. *First:* do people worship God unselfishly, or only for the benefits they believe in or hope for? *Second:* when people suffer, what is going on and where is God? I believe these questions are best kept separate.

The *first* question is handled in prose over a couple of chapters at the start of the book and about half a chapter at the end. God is portrayed in it behaving badly; Job comes out of it with flying colors (1:20–22; 2:10). The *second* question is handled in poetry, as there is great feeling to be expressed; it stretches over almost forty chapters as the core of the book. Retribution theology (the good rewarded, the wicked punished) is assumed by the characters in the book. It is not the central question of the book; held by the friends, it is dismissed by God.

The *first* of the two questions is asked by the satan. Says God: "Have you seen Job? Splendid chap." Says the satan-figure: "Does Job fear God for nothing?" (Less formally: does all right out of it, don't he?) The passage is often described as archaic, an old and traditional tale. The way it is told, it is clearly set in a stylized and archaic setting. But the question is painfully real for any of us today: do we love God unselfishly, or because one way or another we do well out of it—or hope to?

The *second* question is asked by Job. The first part of the text provides the setting: Job is on his rubbish heap, feeling thoroughly sorry for himself. So his question: "Why did I not die at birth?...Why is light given to one in misery, and life to the bitter in soul?" (3:11, 20). In various forms, it has been asked by thinkers through the ages.

The book gives a clear answer to the *first* question: "Yes, we humans can love God unselfishly." Would that the book gave an equally straightforward answer to the *second* question, but it does not. It settles for the claim of mystery, without blame or hostility; it banishes some common and unhelpful answers. The response of mystery is in speeches given to God and addressed directly to Job (38:1—41:34). The unhelpful answers are banished in a short speech given to God and addressed to Eliphaz on behalf of the three: they were wrong and Job was not (42:7–9).

Following Job's passionate lament (chapter 3), the three trot out the traditional answers that are still around today and that don't help us at all. "None of us is perfect, Job; you've surely done something to deserve it." You are surely to blame. "Hang in there, Job; it will be all right in the end. In the meantime, put your trust in God." Ironic, when we think that in the story it was God who gave the satan-figure a free hand. "The wicked always get their comeuppance; that's the way it is, Job. If you're not wicked, you'll be OK in the end." If you are not to blame, then be grateful because it will all come out well in the end. "Don't blame God for it"; count on it, "you deserved much worse." No harm in having that lot given the flick. Job resists them vehemently. A poem on wisdom closes off the exchanges (chapter 28). A final discourse from Job himself brings his words to an end (29:1—31:40).

Elihu comes on the scene without prior introduction. He angrily lambastes both Job and the three (which may be why he does not feature in the final adjudication). His is a response from the human plane. Basically, he lauds the greatness and transcendence of God; whatever detracts from God is wrong.

The response given God, from the whirlwind or storm wind, takes a different tack (38:1—41:34). Its opening—"Who is this that darkens counsel by words without knowledge?"—implies criticism ("darkens," "without knowledge") and addresses Job alone ("this" is singular; 38:2). The speeches deal with what God does and Job cannot do—"Job, where were you?...Have you done?...Do you know?" Basically, Job is out of his depth in his search for clarity (cf. especially 31:35–37). Blame or hostility are absent. At the end, Job accepts the criticism: "I have uttered what I did not understand, things too wonderful for me which I did not know" (42:3). The response given God is from the divine plane. Unlike Elihu, it is not about God; it is about human limitedness.

The tone of the divine speeches (38:1—41:34) is inescapably ambiguous—whether omnipotent/transcendent, or overwhelming/bullying, or insight-generating/caring, and so on. In many ways, how readers hear Job's final words will depend on how they have experienced the tone of these speeches. Their inherent openness as to tone means readers' experience of them is likely to be influenced by factors beyond the text itself. The understanding of God that Job may have come to (as is perhaps the case for Jonah also), if it were touching on the sublime, may perhaps be better not imprisoned in words—left mysterious yet life-giving.

In his conclusion to the exchange with God (42:1–6), Job says: "Now my eye sees you" (42:5). In the book, he hasn't seen anyone, not since Elihu lapsed into silence. The text has had God speak, not appear; "the Lord answered Job out of the whirlwind and said [= Hebrew]" (38:1). Job has just been listening to about four chapters of divine discourse. What is this sight? What might this mean? The physicality of "my eye" does not sit well with insight alone. The text, like its topic, is obscure; it conceals rather than reveals. Avenues toward an understanding include (a) accepting an appearance (or equivalent) as part of God's speaking from the storm, or (b) accepting the incomprehensible vastness of God accountable for so much beyond the vagaries of human life, or (c) accepting a move for Job's experience of God from mediated (indirect; via another) to unmediated (direct; personal). "Hearing of the ear" [literal Hebrew] would normally imply a report of someone else's experience, while seeing with "my eye" would definitely imply one's own experience. As avenues, they are possible; in the context, they are perhaps the best we can do.

The end of the book has God say to Eliphaz, as representative of the three: "You have not spoken of me what is right, as my servant Job has" (42:7, 8). We can be comfortable that the friends were wrong. We may be puzzled as to where Job spoke about God what was right; it is more what Job said about himself that was right. The views held by the friends, justifying God and demeaning Job, are deemed wrong. Job's rightness must be contrasted here with the error of the friends. God's judgment that Job spoke rightly reflects Job's exchanges with the three; it is not about Job's response to God. It relates best to Job's integrity and his refusal to accept the views about God implicit in what is expressed by the three.

The complexity associated with the meaning of the text may mirror the complexity associated with the understanding of the issue. God's discourse, with the wide sweep of its issues and concerns, claims mystery beyond the human capacity to grasp. In a brief adjudication given God (42:7–9), the views of the three are dismissed, baloney unfit for human consumption; the stance of Job is endorsed.

Structurally, 42:1–6 concludes the exchange with God, accepting mystery and situating Job in relationship with God; 42:7–9 concludes the exchanges with the three, having God adjudicate clearly in Job's favor. Beyond doubt: first, against the three, Job holds to his innocence and integrity; second, God declares for Job.

The three have produced explanations for Job's suffering; basically they have blamed Job for it, a view vigorously rejected by him. The discourse given God emphasizes human limitation. Job admits this limitedness (42:3) and the text reports a changed situation (42:5; for 42:6, see the note next page). Job's "and now" or "but now" implies something new, a change. Job's "my eye sees you" implies a relationship—and spells out nothing. The nature of Job's seeing may escape readers' interpretation of the text; something of the kind may not be out of reach of believers' own experience of life. In the text, without a specific theophany, Job's encounter with God does not claim an experience that is peculiar to Job; it does not exclude the possibility for others of some such perception, seeing God differently. The three, who defended God by blaming Job, are declared not to have spoken rightly of God. Job, who rejected the friends' view of God and who refused to accept blame for his situation, is declared to have spoken rightly. Inadequate theology is inadequate. Relationship with God in suffering is possible.

God is given two responses, at quite different levels: one of more than four chapters, addressed to Job; one of three verses, addressed to Eliphaz. *At a primary level,* in two speeches—spoken to Job, reflecting his complaints about his suffering—Job is corrected by God (38:2) and the correction is accepted by Job (42:3). The first speech given God (38:1—39:30) emphasizes divine transcendence over against human limitedness, personified in Job. The second speech (40:6—41:34) addresses the folly of achieving an esteem for human worth by disparaging God (40:8). *At another level,* a second short response—spoken to Eliphaz, reflecting the exchanges between Job and the three friends—has God reject the views of the three and strongly affirm the stance of Job (42:7–9).

The ending of the book, troubling in itself, portrays Job in favorable relationship with God (42:10–17). A comprehensive answer to the issues associated with suffering is not within human reach; the pain of personal suffering does not reflect estrangement from God.

(**Note:** readers need to be aware of the rich ambiguity of both verses 42:5 and 42:6. *Without acknowledging it,* most translations give an "emended" version of 42:6. It has long been known that—without emendation, without input from elsewhere, such as context or tradition—the first part of the verse *cannot* mean "I despise myself," "I disown what I have said," or some such equivalent. Modern studies increasingly recognize that the two verbs in the first part of the verse may both bear on the two objects in the second part. So it is possible that the translation may be along the lines of literally "I repudiate and am of changed mind about dust and ashes"; as an exit line, more freely, "I back off and I've had enough of all this ash-heap stuff." It is highly unlikely that—with the possible exception of Job's demand for clear explanation—the tenor of an entire book, especially this one, would be reversed in one obscure final verse.)

REFLECTIVE MOMENTS
FOR PART SIX

Ezekiel's vision of the valley of dry bones coming to life is a ghoulish scene. Nevertheless, it had potential for immense meaning to the people of Israel who were prisoners of despair—"our hope is lost; we are cut off completely" (37:11). Does faith in God have meaning for me in my moments of hopelessness?

Ezekiel's river is unreal. Whoever heard of "fresh fruit every month" (47:12)? Belief in God's love for us is unreal. Whoever heard of a God, creator of our unbelievably vast universe, who could love us? Could faith, water that "flows from the sanctuary," be so generative?

Jonah is portrayed knowing that God was gracious and merciful, abounding in steadfast love, ready to relent from punishing. Do I believe that? It made Jonah angry enough to give up on life; it devalued his prophecy; it made his world chaotic. What about my own faith and my own world?

The picture of Job is a stylized exaggeration of human suffering, but we know where the picture is right and where we suffer. Have we let go of the answers of the "friends"? Do we accept Job's different vision, even though he has no words for it? Do we have a faith in God, a relationship with God, mature enough to go beyond blame and guilt?

Reflective Activity

Highlight what strikes you as key words in the above reflections. Prioritize them. Choose the first half of your list. Use these to create a poem. Give your poem a title and sub-title. What is evoked in you as you read the poem aloud?

Epilogue: Visions of the Future

Three notable passages look to Israel's future and address our present. All three are priestly writings (from around the time of Israel's exile); all three are visionary, concerned for Israel's future; all three concern our own understanding of biblical text.

The first passage—fragmented and most extensive of the three—is made up of the chapters about the tent sanctuary commanded by God at Mount Sinai, built there under the direction of Moses, and to be situated at the center of the tribes of Israel. The great march of the tribes moves on from Sinai, with the sanctuary at the center, but without arriving at any destination, much less a definitive one—not even on the end of the first day. The detailed description of departure (Num 10:12–28) is nowhere followed by an equivalent description of arrival. The importance needed to account for such a large amount of text (some seventeen chapters—Exod 25—31; 35—40 and Num 1—2; 9—10) relates to three factors: (1) the sanctuary was to enable God to dwell in Israel's midst; (2) it was to enable God to journey with Israel, leading and guiding Israel's journey; (3) it was outside the land of Canaan. To Israel's priestly exiles, all three factors were vital. The tent-sanctuary, however, was never a historical reality; it was a visionary idealization, or imagined ideal, concerned with God's presence among Israel's people, wherever they might be.

The second passage is in the Book of Ezekiel, who was priest as well as prophet. It is Ezekiel 48, the last chapter of the book, following both the vision of the great life-giving river flowing from the temple and the new boundaries for Israel mandated by the Lord God. It specifies the locations of the twelve tribes north and south of the portion for the centrally located sanctuary. Never a reality, it is a visionary idealization concerned with God's presence in the midst of the tribes in the land.

The third passage is Leviticus 25, located toward the end of the book between the Books of Exodus and Numbers; it is devoted to the laws for the Sabbath and jubilee years, presented as commanded by God to Moses, specifically on Mount Sinai. We have no evidence that any such practice of the jubilee ever happened in ancient Israel, no expression of concern about failure to comply with it. Like Ezekiel 48, the project of law in Leviticus 25 is a visionary idealization, looking to some way of regularly restoring a base for equality of opportunity in the future life of Israel. (For further but limited detail, see Campbell and O'Brien, *Rethinking the Pentateuch*, 90–93.)

When we ponder these, the possibility is conceivable that the whole priestly complex at Sinai (treated at length from Exod 25, through all of Leviticus, and through Num 10), concerned the national community that some among Israel's exiles hoped would come about on their return to their land after the Babylonian exile, an expression of hope placed at Sinai, back at the beginning before the portrayal of Israel's first entry into its land.

What is immensely important for us as we ponder Israel's stories is the realization that Israel, confronted with catastrophe, shaped its understanding of God in the light of what had happened. Israel's theologians envisaged a future with God. There would be stories to come.

Postscript: Event and Text

When reading the Bible, we can too easily be distracted by the event, which can lead to serious misunderstandings. We—readers, commentators, users—can go to great lengths to reconstruct in our minds what might have happened. Often, we do it so discreetly and so matter-of-factly that we do not realize we are doing it at all. Of course the text is telling us about an event, and so of course we use our imaginations to recover something of the event. It does not occur to us that the text might be better understood by listening to the text and not worrying about the event.

The matter is less one of historicity than of literary genre, deciding between report and story; often reaching a decision is not easy and must frequently be subjective. Events can generate reports; they can also generate stories. Reports detail events; stories unfold plots and explore meaning. Report and story should not be confused, but often such confusion is not easily avoided. Pointers to the presence of story can be, in general, the configuration of information that is felt to suit the context of story better than that of report. Among specific aspects would be the noting of variant possibilities, the existence of conflicting traditions, the absence of names and dates, or errors with regard to such issues, the absence of expected information or the presence of unexpected information, the inclusion of events that may be thought unlikely (without being in the class we might call the "meaningfully miraculous"), the capacity for opening up questions and leaving them open, and more.

Three examples will have to do. At the Sea, coming out of Egypt (Exod 14), a couple of miracles are no problem; two accounts blended in the text—one with deliverance and a crossing of the Sea and the other with deliverance but no crossing—do invite the reader to attend to the text rather than the event. At the capture of Jericho (Josh 6), mighty walls tumbling down at Israel's shout are no problem; a siege and a king at the start only, trumpets being blown and silence being kept in the middle, the signal and shout happening twice at the end do invite the reader to attend to the text rather than the event. Finally, with the nameless prophets at Bethel (1 Kgs 13), the collapsed altar might belong with a report; what follows, around the lunch and the stay-put donkey and lion, is much more the stuff of story.

In the context of science, there is a relevant parable from the great nineteenth-century physicist, J. C. Maxwell: "In an ordinary belfry, each bell has one rope which comes down through a hole in the floor to the bellringer's room. But suppose that each rope, instead of acting on one bell, contributes to the motion of many pieces of machinery, and that the motion of each piece is determined not by the motion of one rope alone, but by that of several, and suppose, further, that all of this machinery is silent and utterly unknown to the men at the ropes, who can only see as far as the holes in the floor above them" (quoted from Martin Krieger, *Doing Physics,* x–xi). Adapting the image to form criticism: in a report, it is as if each bell has one rope, which acts directly on it; in a story, the link between bells and ropes may be more complex. In a story, the *text* is always in the bellringers' room; the *events* are in the room above.

Again and again, the text cries out for interpretation—not the event.

Index of Scripture Passages

(Scripture passages are listed according to the Hebrew sequence to remind us Gentiles that the Hebrew canon is not in the same order as our Christian canon).

First Samuel
15	71–73
17	55–58, 66

Second Samuel
11—12	58–60, 66
12	73–75
13	60–61, 66
15—19	62–64, 67
20	64–66, 67

First Kings
13	79–80
21	75–77
22	80–82

Isaiah
5	98–100

Jeremiah
2	96–98
7	90–92
26	100–2
28	82–84
36	103–5

Ezekiel
37	108–10
47	110–12
48	124

Hosea
1	92–94
11	94–96

Amos
3	86–88
7—9	88–90

Jonah
	112–15

Psalms
8	9
74	9, 11
104	8, 10

Job
	115–20
26	9
38	9, 10

Proverbs
8	8–9, 10